Typology of knowledge, skills and competences: clarification of the concept and prototype

Jonathan Winterton

Françoise Delamare - Le Deist

Emma Stringfellow

Cedefop Reference series; 64

Luxembourg: Office for Official Publications of the European Communities, 2006

A great deal of additional information on the European Union is available on the Internet.
It can be accessed through the Europa server (http://europa.eu).

Cataloguing data can be found at the end of this publication.

Luxembourg: Office for Official Publications of the European Communities, 2006

ISBN 92-896-0427-1
ISSN 1608-7089

Printed in Italy

The **European Centre for the Development
of Vocational Training** (Cedefop) is the European Union's
reference centre for vocational education and training.
We provide information on and analyses of vocational
education and training systems, policies, research and practice.
Cedefop was established in 1975
by Council Regulation (EEC) No 337/75.

Europe 123
GR-57001 Thessaloniki (Pylea)

Postal Address: PO Box 22427
GR-55102 Thessaloniki

Tel. (30) 23 10 49 01 11
Fax (30) 23 10 49 00 20
E-mail: info@cedefop.europa.eu
Homepage: www.cedefop.europa.eu
Interactive website: www.trainingvillage.gr

Edited by: **Cedefop**
Sellin Burkart, *Project manager*

Published under the responsibility of:
Aviana Bulgarelli, *Director*
Christian Lettmayr, *Deputy Director*

Foreword

This study was commissioned by Cedefop from the centre for European research in employment and human resources at Toulouse business school on behalf of the credit transfer technical working group. This group was set up by the European Commission in 2003 in the framework of the Copenhagen process on enhanced cooperation in vocational education and training. Cedefop supports this and other working groups with studies, advice, expertise and its communication tools (see *inter alia* http://communities.trainingvillage.gr/credittransfer).

The brief was to clarify concepts, investigate classifications and typologies applied in Member States and advise the working group on descriptors for learning outcomes. Finally, a prototype typology applicable for credit accumulation and transfer should be developed as a practical result. The study presented by the authors is an academic exercise which is useful but difficult to translate into policy action. It helped identify gaps in existing tools and instruments for describing learning outcomes in an internationally comparative and context-independent way.

The use of the term 'competence' is shown to be particularly ambiguous and applicable to various situations with different meanings. This term needs careful specification and interpretation if it is to be properly understood. Countries or regions have their own definition of competence and each sector or occupational family has its own interpretation. Outcomes of learning cannot be described by using this term only. We have to add knowledge and skills or, as the authors propose, use terms such as cognitive competence, functional competence or meta-competence, understood as personal and social-attitudinal competence, to encompass the necessary knowledge and skills.

It was also confirmed that sector specific or occupational classifications at European level are currently insufficiently specified, e.g. to describe in more detail the learning outcomes relating to credit delivery and access for further education or training and working life or employment. A more detailed typology or register of jobs and occupational activities is fundamental for establishing a comprehensive European credit transfer system. Such a register has to be developed with the assistance of sector experts and professionals from the respective occupational groups and may have to be propagated by European level social partner organisations. Human resource and training experts alone are not able to specify these categories. A dictionary of job titles or European jobs register linked to short abstracts in all European languages could substantially support both the European employment strategy and the intended lifelong learning strategy. This task could be undertaken by the European Commission's employment and social affairs department in close contact with the statistical office Eurostat; it goes beyond the mandate of Cedefop and training experts.

This study's outcomes complement the earlier study on reference levels by a research team from the UK Qualifications and Curriculum Agency, made available in 2005 by Cedefop (see also: http://communities.trainingvillage.gr/credittransfer). The study thus supports the working group's efforts towards agreeing common descriptors on outcomes of learning and for assisting national training providers to reach common agreements on units and modules of training around which they intend to exchange students and trainees and to agree the amount of credits to be delivered jointly. Both studies substantially support more recent efforts of the European Commission and Member States to come to an agreement on an overarching 'European qualifications framework' for fully implementing joint actions for transparency and recognition of qualifications built on common trust and quality assurance in the face of major social and economic challenges.

Thessaloniki, March 2005

Stavros Stavrou
Deputy Director

Burkart Sellin
Project manager

Table of contents

List of tables and figures

1. Executive summary

This report is one in a series launched by the European Commission and Cedefop to support the work of the Copenhagen process technical working group (TWG) on credit transfer established in November 2002. The TWG developed proposals for the principles of a European credit transfer system for VET (ECVET), endorsed in December 2004 by the Maastricht communiqué, which underlines the need for ECVET to be compatible with the European credit transfer system (ECTS) in higher education. Within the overall European qualifications framework (EQF) proposed by the Maastricht communiqué, ECVET and ECTS should share a set of common reference levels for qualifications. These common reference levels should be described by learning outcomes and expressed in competences, providing a reading grid that makes it possible to compare different learning outcomes and the relationships between them.

Developing the vertical axis of the grid – the common reference levels – has been the subject of another study commissioned by Cedefop and undertaken by a team from the UK Qualifications and Curriculum Authority. Assessing existing credit transfer systems in VET and their applicability to ECVET was the subject of a second study commissioned by Cedefop and undertaken by colleagues at Kassel University. This third report commissioned by Cedefop focuses on the horizontal dimension of the grid, a typology of learning outcomes about knowledge, skills and competences (KSCs).

This executive summary outlines: the methodology adopted; the key concepts of KSCs; issues on using typologies of KSCs; European experience in using KSCs; a report on these approaches as the basis for the prototype typology; and some broad conclusions and recommendations for further development.

Methodology

As a starting point, a comprehensive literature review was undertaken to explore approaches to typologies and frameworks of KSCs through Internet searches, EU and national policy documentation and the work of EU and national sector VET bodies. Subsequent analyses of different approaches to knowledge, skills and competence were circulated to members of the Cedefop ReferNet and VET experts through the European HRD network. They were also presented to the TWG in Brussels, at the European symposium *La construction de qualifications européennes* held at the European Parliament in Strasbourg in September 2004 and at the Workshop on European credit transfer system in vocational training held at *Wissenschaftszentrum*, Bonn in October 2004. A parallel paper exploring approaches to competence was presented at the fifth conference on HRD research and practice in Limerick in May 2004 which benefited from feedback from anonymous referees before publication in *Human resource development international*, in March 2005. The arguments have had considerable exposure to expert critique and evaluation and experts have had ample opportunity to contribute to the discussion.

The concepts underpinning KSCs

The report traces the concepts underpinning KSCs, noting that these relate to learning outcomes or outputs, irrespective of acquisition routes of involved, rather than on learning inputs. Developing an appropriate typology of KSCs is important in promoting labour mobility in three senses: vertical as in career progression; horizontal as in movement between sectors; and spatial, as in mobility in the enlarged EU. Such a focus also offers potential for integrating formal education and training with informal and experiential development, essential to fulfil the objectives of the EU lifelong learning strategy, widening access to learning and development and providing 'ladders' for those having had fewer opportunities for formal education and training but having none the less developed KSCs experientially.

Cognitive learning, related to understanding and using new concepts, may be contrasted with behavioural learning, related to the physical ability to act. These are sometimes associated with stages in learning but such an approach fails to recognise the importance of interaction between cognitive and behavioural learning and does not elaborate the mechanisms by which individual learning becomes organisational learning. More widely accepted cyclical models of learning illustrate the links between two types of learning: 'single-loop' learning about obtaining knowledge to solve specific problems based on existing premises; and 'double-loop' learning about establishing new premises such as mental models and perspectives.

Underlying intellectual abilities are prerequisites for acquiring KSCs even though intelligence cannot be taken as a proxy for KSCs despite its predictive power in relation to ability to acquire these attributes. There are various approaches to measuring intelligence, and while in the work context aspects such as practical intelligence, social intelligence and emotional intelligence are often viewed as essential, these are less amenable to evaluation and more controversial than traditional psychometric measures.

Knowledge is sometimes viewed as if it were a concrete manifestation of abstract intelligence, but it is actually the result of an interaction between intelligence (capacity to learn) and situation (opportunity to learn), so is more socially-constructed than intelligence. Knowledge includes theory and concepts, as well as tacit knowledge gained as a result of the experience of performing certain tasks. Understanding refers to more holistic knowledge of processes and contexts and may be distinguished as know-why, as opposed to know-that. Know-how is often associated with tacit knowledge and know-that with propositional knowledge, reflected in the distinction between declarative knowledge (knowing what), and procedural knowledge (knowing how). From this perspective, it is often argued that acquiring declarative knowledge (explicit factual knowledge) must precede developing procedural knowledge, which relates to using knowledge in context.

Skill is usually used to refer to a level of performance, in the sense of accuracy and speed in performing particular tasks (skilled performance). Skilled performance has long been a subject of psychological studies, which consider both physical psychomotor abilities and mental cognitive abilities. The early finding that (diminishing marginal) improvement in performance appears to continue indefinitely has generally been confirmed in later research, which led to the conclusion that learning can be described as a linear function of the logarithms of times and trials. Recent skill research has included broader cognitive skills such as problem-solving and decision-making, demonstrating the difficulty in regarding such cognitive competences as knowledge rather than skill. Skill has been defined as: goal-directed, well-organised behaviour that is acquired through practice and performed with economy of effort.

Competence is a term subject to such diverse use and interpretation that it is impossible to identify or impute a coherent theory or to arrive at a definition capable of accommodating and reconciling all the different ways the term is used. After exploring the different interpretations, the common position is that if intellectual capabilities are required to develop knowledge and operationalising knowledge is part of developing skills, all are prerequisites to developing competence and other social and attitudinal skills.

Use of typologies of KSCs

Recent developments in the use of typologies of KSCs and some of the problems in relation to generic KSCs are considered, along with alternative interpretative approaches and the notions of expertise and higher order work.

An influential generic typology of KSCs was developed by Bloom and colleagues from the 1960s for use in educational establishments. Generally known as Bloom's taxonomy, it is based on three domains of educational activities: cognitive, affective and psychomotor (which was added later). The cognitive domain relates to mental skills (knowledge), the affective domain for growth in feelings or emotional areas (attitudes), while the psychomotor domain is concerned with manual or physical skills (skills). This taxonomy is influential in the training world and trainers frequently refer to these as KSA (knowledge, skills and attitudes). Bloom's taxonomy has strongly influenced development of the Irish qualifications framework.

Use of generic KSC typologies and frameworks in enterprises, as opposed to education, has been promoted by efforts to link development to organisational strategy and to retain core competence as a key source of competitive advantage. There is an apparent paradox in this, since if concentrating on core competences distinctive and specific to each individual organisation is what gives competitive advantage, the scope for generic frameworks is limited.

Strategies emphasising core competence as a key organisational resource are prevalent in the management literature of the 1990s, which argues that the key to competitive advantage lies in the capacity within the organisation for developing and maintaining core competence. Competency modelling is about identifying the critical success factors driving performance in organisations and competence assessment is concerned with determining the extent to which individuals have these critical competencies.

The idea that generic KSCs are transferable across different knowledge domains has been widely questioned and regarded as mechanistic and reductionist. Since most definitions of KSCs are centred on the individual, these are viewed as independent of the social and task-specific context in which performance occurs, but the level of skill is a characteristic not only of a person but also of a context; people do not have competences independent of context. In recognition of this, a constructivist approach to defining competence has arisen, where it is argued that competence is governed by the context in which it is applied. The rationalist approach of operationalising attributes into quantitative measures has equally been criticised for creating abstract, overly narrow and simplified descriptions of competence that fail adequately to reflect the complexity of competence in work performance. Alternative, interpretative approaches, derived from phenomenology, see competence not as a duality but as worker and work forming one entity through experience of work.

Improvements in performance continue until performance reaches a level that can be considered expert. Experts have been found to display a greater capacity to invoke and refine schemas of interpretation and deeper recognition-triggered reasoning, than novices who do little more than attempt a literal perceptual interpretation. While innate abilities are important in developing expertise, the special characteristics that define expertise are usually specific to that domain, suggesting that practice is more important, although certain characteristics appear to apply to experts in a range of domains. Conceptual competences, including both cognitive and meta-competences are often associated with higher level jobs involving more responsibility, although there is evidence that all workers become more effective when they reflect on their actions at work. This notion is reinforced with an interpretative approach capable of incorporating tacit skills and knowledge. Elliott Jacques devised a measure of the level of work roles by the 'time-span of discretion' (the longest targeted completion time for any of the tasks assigned), which he proposed as an alternative to job evaluation techniques. Jacques's categorisation of levels of jobs by responsibility influenced the determination of reference levels for ECVET.

European experience with KSCs

Given the different traditions of VET systems and economic conditions between EU Member States, it is understandable that there is currently no common approach to defining learning outcomes by KSCs. The report reviews some of the approaches and recent developments relevant to establishing a common typology of KSCs.

The United Kingdom was the first to adopt a competence-based approach to VET to establish a nation-wide unified system of work-based qualifications in the 1980s. The vocational qualifications created under the new framework were based on occupational standards of competence, grounded in functional analysis of occupations in various contexts. Emphasis is on functional competence and ability to perform to the standards required of employment in a work context. Occupational standards are written as statements of competence, describing good practice needed in the workplace rather than individual attributes. Key roles are identified and broken down into units of competence. These are further subdivided into elements of competence and for each element, performance criteria are defined which form the basis for assessment, with range indicators provided for guidance. Vocational qualifications have been criticised for their apparent lack of adequate theoretical foundation and insufficient attention to social issues at work. While the main approach in the United Kingdom remains one of functional competence, some employers adopted other generic models or created hybrid models incorporating functional competences and psycho-social characteristics.

In France, the continued challenge of restructuring enterprises towards the end of the 1980s led the ANPE (*Agence nationale pour l'emploi*) to launch ROME (*Répertoire opérationnel des métiers et des emplois*) which was modified in 1993 and gave a central role to competence. The *Gestion prévisionnelle des emplois et des compétences* (GPEC) was developed to accompany organisational transformation in which human resources came to be viewed as a source of competitive advantage. GPEC evolved into *emplois types en dynamique* (ETED) as a method that explicitly recognises the rapidity of changes in competence requirements. In the 1990s, the state introduced a right for individuals to have a *bilan de compétences* undertaken to provide a basis for personal development in their occupation. The *Objectif competences* initiative, launched by the employers' association MEDEF (*Mouvement des Entreprises de France*) in 2002, provided extensive practical information on the use of competence within enterprises. The French approach is more comprehensive than the British, considering *savoir* (*compétences théoriques*, i.e. knowledge), *savoir-faire* (*compétences pratiques*, i.e. functional competences) and *savoir-être* (*compétences sociales et comportementales*, i.e. behavioural competencies). There is a strong concordance between the United Kingdom use of functional competence and the French *savoir-faire* and between the US use of soft competences and the French *savoir-être*.

The German dual system of VET has long been viewed as a model for Europe and has had a determining influence on Hungary, Austria and Slovenia and, to a lesser extent, the Scandinavian countries. While competence (*Kompetenz*) was implicit in the system, the main emphasis was on specifying the necessary learning inputs, rather than outcomes, to master a trade. Occupational competence is rooted in the concept of *Beruf* (usually translated as occupation, but encompassing the traditions of the craft from the trade and craft guilds), which defines vocational training theory and associated pedagogy. During the 1960s, qualification (*Qualifikation*) was understood not as possessing a certificate but as mastery of specific life-situations or occupational tasks. The concept of key qualifications (*Schlüsselqualifikationen*) was introduced in the 1980s, and still dominates today. While *Qualifikation* signifies the ability to master concrete (generally professional) situation requirements (so is clearly application-oriented), *Kompetenz* refers to the capacity of a person to act, is subject-oriented and is more holistic, comprising not only content or subject knowledge and ability, but also extra-subject or transversal abilities (often still described as *Schlüsselqualifikationen* but increasingly also as *Methodenkompetenz, Sozialkompetenz, Personalkompetenz*). During the 1980s, the term *Kompetenz* was further differentiated so that more or less all facets of training were stylised to independent competences, such as media-competence (*Medienkompetenz*), ecological-competence (*ökologische Kompetenz*) and democracy-competence (*Demokratiekompetenz*). In 1996, the German education system adopted an action competence (*Handlungskompetenz*) approach, moving from subject (inputs) to competence (outcomes) and curricula specifying learning fields (*Lernfelder*) rather than occupation related knowledge and skills content. The standard typology of competences adopted in 2000 appears at the beginning of every new vocational training curriculum, elaborating vocational action competence (*Handlungskompetenz*) by domain or subject-competence (*Fachkompetenz*), personal competence (*Personalkompetenz*) and social competence (*Sozialkompetenz*). General cognitive competence (*Sachkompetenz*), the ability to think and act in an insightful and problem-solving way, is a prerequisite for developing *Fachkompetenz*, which therefore includes both cognitive and functional competences.

In recent years many other Member States have moved towards learning outcomes and competence-based VET systems and qualifications, sometimes following closely one of the above models and occasionally developing distinctive approaches. Competence-based occupational profiles and/or qualification frameworks already exist or are under development in most of the 15 original EU Member States and are being promoted in those of the 10 new EU Member States that had not already adopted such an approach. Several of these are also considered in the report and compared with the three approaches described in detail.

A prototype typology of KSCs

As the review has shown a growing influence of multi-dimensional frameworks of KSCs, a unified typology of KSCs is proposed, drawing upon perceived good practice within the EU. The holistic approach to competence combining knowledge, skills and attitudes is gaining ground over narrower approaches and several authorities are developing more integrated approaches along these lines. Where interpretive approaches have also been influential, competence is viewed as being multifaceted, holistic and integrated. Such an approach offers a unifying framework for defining the KSCs that is necessary for particular occupations and provides a starting point for establishing a typology of KSCs for the ECVET. The three dimensions, cognitive, functional and social competences, are fairly universal and are clearly consistent with the French approach (*savoir*, *savoir faire*, *savoir être*) as well as the longstanding KSA (knowledge, skills and attitudes) of the training profession derived from Bloom's taxonomy of learning. Given the TWG decision to retain 'knowledge, skills and competences' (KSCs) as a unified statement, meta-competencies have been retained within the social competences category. Competence is too broad a term without further qualification: in the United Kingdom and Ireland competence is generally understood as the ability to show at work, the necessary skills (functional competences), usually with appropriate basic knowledge (cognitive competences) and sometimes appropriate social competences (behavioural and attitudinal competences). By incorporating meta-competencies with social ones the horizontal dimension is consistent with the work of the TWG to date, but using the term competence as a short-hand for social competence is potentially problematic because the term is most commonly used as an umbrella term for demonstrating requisite knowledge and skills as well as appropriate behaviour in a work context. It is therefore strongly recommended that in the interests of analytical precision, ECVET adopts the terminology of cognitive competence, functional competence and social competence.

The outline of the broad typology of KSCs represents a starting point for developing a prototype typology of learning outcomes for ECVET. Using such a framework of learning outcomes, educational and work-based provision can be more closely aligned, exploiting the synergy between formal education and experiential learning to develop professional competence. However, for the typology to be of practical use there is a major task of assessing the extent to which existing typologies of learning outcomes and qualifications frameworks can be accommodated within such an overall typology, when considered in more detail. To make the typology operational, national and sector frameworks must therefore be examined in more detail to test the practical potential of the typology of KSCs in specific sectors and occupations. The agreed overall architecture has eight vertical reference levels and three broad horizontal descriptors. Selected frameworks can be used to populate the matrix with a series of specific descriptors for the occupation or sector, but not all levels will be appropriate in a given sector or occupational group; equally some KSC horizontal dimensions may not feature at all in some cases (although most would be expected to have some requirements in all three dimensions). To test the utility of the prototype typology it is necessary to explore the scope for integrating existing classifications at international, national and sector levels. The amount of detail in descriptors of what someone should know, what they should be able to do and how they should behave, to be considered competent at a particular level in a particular occupation, must also be agreed. If the typology is underspecified it risks insufficient precision to be operable; if it is overspecified it risks becoming unusable and more difficult to establish zones of common trust within each part of the matrix.

The national qualifications frameworks introduced in Ireland and Scotland are particularly important as they have established levels that integrate VET and HE, thus under the Bologna-Copenhagen process joined up lifelong learning is possible. The Scottish framework has 12 levels and the Irish framework 10, in contrast with the 8 levels agreed as European reference levels. The question of fitting existing national levels into the European structure is amenable to resolution through approximation and will necessarily be subject to further discussion but for the present purposes it is necessary to compare the general horizontal descriptors in these frameworks and explore the extent to which they can be accommodated in the prototype typology of KSCs.

There is broad consensus between the countries considered to date at the level of the three dimensions associated with the KSCs typology, but the fit is not perfect. In some cases the differences can be put down largely to terminology. In Ireland, separating competence and context (applying knowledge and skills), can be viewed as supporting the idea that it is not simply knowledge and skills that matter but their application in a workplace context. This is largely implicit in the approaches of France, Portugal, Finland and the United Kingdom (England and Wales). In several cases, the differences appear to be fundamental and conceptual. In the German model, separating general cognitive abilities (*Sachkompetenz*) from domain-specific knowledge and skills (*Fachkompetenz*) is paralleled in the Scottish differentiation of generic cognitive skills from knowledge and understanding appropriate for the occupation. The Scottish model also separates generic skills (communication, numeracy, IT) from what is essentially domain-specific practice. However, in the German model, the further breaking down of specific processes (*Methodenkompetenz*) and behaviours (*Sozialkompetenz* relating both to social competence and appropriate functional behaviour), is more difficult to reconcile with other approaches, even if it better reflects the reality of the totality of work.

Little progress was made on incorporating occupational competence and qualifications frameworks. Initially it was intended to consider a 'sunset industry' (steel or clothing); a high knowledge-based sector (pharmaceuticals or ICT); a strategic manufacturing industry (engineering or aerospace); a service sector (health); and a transversal occupational group (managers). This proved overambitious with the time and resources available and the report only explores using the prototype typology tentatively against ICT occupations. ICT occupations are interesting because they have developed without the rigidities associated with the sort of regulation that applies to health professions and the traditions of older crafts; every area of economic activity is affected by ICT and the pace of technological change makes these the most dynamic occupations. Hence there has been neither a commonly agreed classification of ICT jobs nor elaboration of the necessary KSCs associated with them. The strategic importance of ICT occupations in the European economy and the highly global character of the ICT sector have resulted in substantial efforts to develop a comprehensive framework of ICT skills. In the United Kingdom (UK), for example, key bodies in ICT, the British computer society, e-skills UK (the sector skills council for ICT), the Institution of Electrical Engineers and the Institute for the Management of Information Systems, formed the SFIA foundation to develop the skills framework for the information age (SFIA). The SFIA is designed to enable organisations to map existing skills and identify skills gaps as well as provide a framework for recruitment, training, assessment and human resource planning. The SFIA was created using the sort of matrix proposed for ECVET, with vertical reference levels relating to levels of responsibility and a horizontal dimension of descriptors relating to areas of work and the range of skills required to undertake the activities. The seven levels correspond well with levels 2-8 in the reference levels agreed for ECVET but the descriptors are areas of activity or tasks (such as systems development management) rather than comprehensive descriptions of the KSCs involved, although these could be mapped to detailed competence descriptors. A Cedefop-funded study has made substantial progress towards defining a European ICT skills framework with five skill levels, summarising the complete European (reference) framework of ICT qualifications for all work areas and subdegree qualification levels. This research into the qualitative ICT skill needs within a range of ICT business areas demonstrates that a new content oriented skill structure is needed to describe and define all ICT skills for each of the five skill levels. The breakdown could be reconciled with the prototype typology. However, such a task must be undertaken by sector specialists at such time as this or another typology is adopted as the horizontal dimension of ECVET.

The report concludes that the challenge of developing a consistent and coherent typology of KSCs is to acknowledge the value of the diversity of approaches and not to prescribe a one-size-fits-all typology unadapted to the needs of a specific labour market or training and education system. This tentative effort to clarify terms and develop a prototype typology of KSCs is limited in both breadth and depth but forms a starting point for developing a comprehensive typology. To establish the typology, further actions are needed, remaining problems need to be addressed and further research is required. The actions needed to establish the typology as the horizontal dimension of a European system of credit transfer must involve the main actors in VET. Ministries and agencies responsible for VET need to ensure that the learning outcomes in national qualification frameworks can use the typology as a template for comparison with other countries. This is not a question of harmonisation, which would be politically unacceptable and unworkable given the different cultures and traditions of VET, but of accommodation to promote transparency. Adopting a competence typology requires flexibility to allow continuous reform and updating of existing qualifications frameworks in response to changes in the external environment. While the need for an overarching competence framework is important for inter-sector and international mobility, much of the detailed work will be at sector level, involving the social partners and sector training bodies. Since sector needs are relatively uniform across different countries, it is at this level the obstacles can and are being overcome. The Leonardo da Vinci programme offers considerable potential, since many Leonardo projects are concerned with creating 'zones of mutual trust' in developing new EU-wide qualifications. It is important that further work is undertaken to harvest the results of these projects and incorporate them in the ECVET work programme. In this way the top-down facilitating typology can act as guide to ensure there is sufficient inter-sector comparability and commonality, while the bottom-up sector level zones of mutual trust ensure relevance to workplace needs.

Perhaps the greatest challenge is that if the objective of creating seamless lifelong learning is to be achieved, the typology of competence adopted in VET must dovetail with learning outcomes in HE. Conceptual problems may also be anticipated from the work completed to date, which has shown the difficulty is not simply in establishing an agreed terminology, but ensuring that a common vocabulary is underpinned by common meaning. The differences in VET systems and cultures present additional difficulties, but the typology must be sufficiently flexible to accommodate this diversity since it would be counterproductive to attempt to harmonise systems that have developed to suit different socioeconomic conditions. Where fundamental conceptual differences are apparent, because of the underlying theoretical models and assumptions, further work is needed to reconcile these and reach a common understanding without imposing a single approach. Further research is required covering all 25 EU Member States and ultimately researching practice beyond Europe. It is necessary to extend the depth of analysis, investigating competence in greater detail in specific occupations. Further work must be undertaken at sector level by sector specialists and we provide some broad occupational frameworks that appear, *prima facie*, to be suitable for testing and operationalising the typology. Two of these are also of importance because the labour force manifests extensive geographic mobility, including between Member States: the health sector (with particular emphasis on nursing) and tourism.

2. Introduction and background

This report is one in a series launched by the European Commission and Cedefop to support the work of the Copenhagen process technical working group (TWG) on credit transfer. The mandate of the TWG comes directly from 'the Copenhagen declaration on enhanced cooperation in vocational education and training' (VET), namely to investigate:

> how transparency, comparability, transferability and recognition of competences and/or qualifications, between different countries and at different levels, could be promoted by developing reference levels, common principles for certification, and common measures, including a credit transfer system for vocational education and training (TWG, 2003, p. 5).

Established in November 2002, the TWG on credit transfer in VET has developed proposals for the principles and rules of a European credit transfer system for VET (ECVET) which should be supported by a common reference levels framework for competences and qualifications (TWG, 2004). Implementing the ECVET system was politically endorsed in December 2004 by the Maastricht communiqué, which underlines the need for the compatibility of ECVET with the European credit transfer system (ECTS) in higher education.

Within the overall European qualifications framework (EQF) proposed by the Maastricht communiqué, ECVET and ECTS should share a set of common reference levels for qualifications. These common reference levels should be described by learning outcomes and expressed in competences, providing a reading grid that makes it possible to compare different learning outcomes and the relationships between them. The first of the essential rules proposed by the credit transfer TWG for ECVET states:

> The objectives of a learning pathway, a VET programme or elements of a qualification are expressed as learning outcomes in terms of knowledge, skills and competences to be acquired and mastered at a given reference level (TWG, 2004, chapter 2.3.1. i).

Developing the vertical axis of the grid – the common reference levels – has been the subject of another study commissioned by Cedefop and undertaken by a team from the UK Qualifications and Curriculum Authority (Coles and Oates, 2004). Assessing existing credit transfer systems in VET and their applicability to ECVET was the subject of the second study commissioned by Cedefop and undertaken by Kassel University (Le Mouillour, 2004).

This report, the third commissioned by Cedefop, focuses on the horizontal dimension of the grid, a typology of learning outcomes by knowledge, skills and competences.

The move towards outcome or competence-based approaches in VET can be seen in most European countries and recognises the need to adopt a more demand-driven model which responds better to the needs of the labour market (Mansfield, 2004, p. 300), and of the importance of adaptive training and work-based learning (Winterton, 2000; Winterton and Winterton, 1997). It also reflects increasing recognition at national and European levels of the importance of informal and non-formal learning (Bjørnåvold, 1997; 1999; 2000; Coffield, 2000). Recognising and validating/certifying informal and non-formal learning – an urgent priority for European and national VET policies and one of the greatest challenges – is inconceivable without an outcome-based approach.

The European credit transfer system (ECTS) in higher education, introduced in 1989, has demonstrated the potential of a credit transfer system for enhancing transferability and mobility and has been given further impetus by the Bologna Declaration of June 1999. The need to create a parallel process for VET has become crucial since the Copenhagen Declaration in November 2002 which committed Member States to increasing cooperation in VET.

At the Laeken European Council in December 2001, the social partners expressed their willingness to improve the effectiveness of social dialogue; in addition to their involvement in the consultation exercise following the *Memorandum on lifelong learning* published by the European Commission in November 2001, they gave a clear commitment to promote lifelong learning policy and practice and to participate in the monitoring and evaluation of progress. Following elaboration of the EU lifelong learning strategy, the social partners agreed, on 28 February 2002, a *Framework of actions for the lifelong development of competencies and qualifications*, in which they identified four priorities:
(a) identification and anticipation of competences and qualifications needs;
(b) recognition and validation of competences and qualifications;
(c) information, support and guidance;
(d) resources (ETUC, UNICE/UEAPME and CEEP, 2002).

In the *Framework of actions* the social partners emphasise the importance of developing a competence-based approach to credit transfer:

> The social partners consider it necessary to deepen dialogue with the aim of improving transparency and transferability, both for the employee and for the enterprise, to facilitate geographical and occupational mobility and to increase the efficiency of labour markets:

- by promoting the development of means of recognition and validation of competencies;
- by providing a system for transferable qualifications;
- by identifying the possible links and complementarities with recognised diplomas.

At European level, social partners will contribute to continuing discussions on transparency and recognition of competencies and qualifications.

In higher education too, there has been a discernible move towards a more outcome-based approach, reflected in the Berlin communiqué of September 2003 which encourages Member States:

> to elaborate a framework of comparable and compatible qualifications for their higher education systems, which should seek to describe qualifications by workload, level, learning outcomes, competences and profile (Bologna working group on qualifications frameworks, 2004).

The report of the Bologna working group on qualifications frameworks for higher education defines learning outcomes as 'statements of what a learner is expected to know, understand and/or be able to do at the end of a period of learning' and points out the need to consider the extent to which common approaches to understanding and defining learning outcomes between countries should be explored. Ideally the horizontal dimension of ECVET – the typology of knowledge, skills and competences – should be applicable in both domains; the academic and VET or lifelong learning domain (¹). However, as the European Commission (2004, p. 5) points out:

> ECTS is a system primarily based on student workload and knowledge required to achieve the objectives of a programme of study. The specificities of VET, more particularly the close and direct links which exist between VET, the labour market and real occupations, require a credit transfer system that is fully, from the outset, a competence-based system.

One of the challenges identified in the first report of the Credit transfer TWG is the semantic differences in the use of the same terms and concepts in national VET systems, which 'reflect important differences in systems, structures and cultural approaches' (TWG, 2003, p. 7). It is against this backgroundthat the

---

(¹) See Cedefop foreword to *European approaches to credit transfer systems in VET* (Le Mouillour, 2004).

need has been identified for a prototype typology of qualitative outcomes of VET by knowledge, skills and competences (KSCs).

The following section outlines the methodology adopted, while Section 3 explores the concepts underpinning KSCs and Section 4 considers issues in the use of typologies of KSCs. Section 5 reviews European experience in the use of KSCs; a synthesis of these approaches forms the basis for the prototype typology developed in Section 6, which is then operationalised by drawing on current practice with national frameworks of KSCs and sector level frameworks. Section 7 offers some broad conclusions relating to recommendations for further research and development.

3. Methodology

The focus of this study is an assessment of existing classifications and typologies of KSCs, at international, national, regional and sectoral levels, identifying for each:
(a) the level of detail of the elements described;
(b) the specificity in terms of application (sector, job, etc.);
(c) the utility of these typologies at European or International level.

Following an analysis and synthesis of the different approaches, the study will develop, for use within the framework of an emerging ECVET system:
(a) a prototype typology of KSCs;
(b) an example of applying the prototype typology;
(c) recommendations for maintenance of the typology.

As a starting point for this work, a comprehensive literature review was undertaken (see References) to explore approaches to typologies and frameworks of KSCs, including in particular the following sources:
(a) academic and practitioner literature, including Internet searches;
(b) policy documentation at EU level and within Member States;
(c) the work of sector VET bodies at EU level and within Member States.

A first analysis of different approaches to knowledge, skills and competence was presented to the TWG meeting in Brussels on 11 May 2004 as an extended project outline. The extended study outline was revised in the light of comments received and then e-mailed to TWG members, Cedefop ReferNet contacts and other VET experts via the UFHRD (including Euresform) and the European HRD network, asking for comments on the recommended framework and details of typologies in use in each country. Detailed responses were obtained from 25 individuals in 14 countries (see details in Annex 1). In parallel, a fuller version of the argument was presented as an academic paper at the University forum for human resource development annual conference in Limerick on 28 May 2004 (Delamare Le Deist and Winterton, 2004). This paper benefited from the comments of anonymous peer reviewers and from interaction with those present at the conference. Further feedback was obtained from anonymous referees in the course of submission of a revised version to *Human resource development international* (Delamare Le Deist and Winterton, 2005). The arguments have had considerable exposure to expert critique and evaluation and there has been ample opportunity for experts to contribute to the discussion. The response rate from ReferNet contacts was low, perhaps reflecting the timing of the enquiry, which straddled the summer vacation.

4. Concepts underpinning knowledge, skills and competences

One of the key virtues of focusing on knowledge, skills and competences is that these relate to learning outcomes or outputs, irrespective of the routes of acquisition involved, rather than on learning inputs. Developing an appropriate typology of KSCs is important in promoting labour mobility in three senses: vertical as in career progression; horizontal as in movement between sectors; and spatial in terms of mobility within the enlarged EU. Such a focus also offers the potential for integrating formal education and training with informal and experiential development, essential to fulfil the objectives of the EU lifelong learning strategy, widening access to learning and development and providing ladders for those who have had fewer opportunities for formal education and training but have none the less developed KSCs experientially.

4.1. Routes of formation and recognition of KSCs

The line between formal and non-formal learning is indistinct (Cullen et al., 2000) and cannot be rigidly defined. However, drawing upon the analytical frameworks developed in the Leonardo da Vinci projects VALID and DEVELOP, four broad routes can be distinguished in terms of the mechanisms through which KSCs are acquired and recognised (Figure 1).

Figure 1: **Routes of formation and recognition of KSCs**

		Recognition	
		uncertified	*certified*
	formal	adaptive	qualified
Acquisition			
	informal	tacit	accredited

The four routes range from tacit KSCs, informally gained and uncertified, to qualified KSCs gained through formal instruction and recognised by certification. Between these extremes are examples of formal instruction that is uncertified, such as adaptive training in connection with product and process changes, and informal experiential learning that is certified through some accreditation process.

Bjørnåvold and Tissot (2000, p. 204-205) offer the further refinement of distinguishing between formal learning (within an organised and structured context), non-formal learning (embedded in planned activities that are not explicitly designated as learning) and informal learning (daily life activities involving experiential or accidental learning). Eraut (2000b, p. 12) argues that the label 'informal learning' is unhelpful if one accepts that 'the majority of human learning does not occur in formal contexts', and advocates distinguishing formal and non-formal *environmental settings*. Following this approach, Straka (2002, p. 156) offers a more sophisticated analysis, distinguishing routes to learning by learning types (explicit, accidental/incidental or implicit) and environmental conditions (formal or non-formal). Importantly, Straka (2002, p. 155) notes that learning types are not only related to particular environmental settings. While explicit learning may predominate in a formal setting and implicit in a non-formal setting, these types of learning are found in each context and accidental learning is just as likely to occur in formal as non-formal conditions. The ECVET model intends however, to encompass both formal and non-formal learning, while starting from formal in the short term and being open to non-formal learning in the medium and longer term.

4.2. Learning processes

In addition to the type of learning and the environmental setting, it is important to consider the actual learning process, and different processes may be associated with developing different aspects of KSCs. The organisational learning and learning organisation literature (Dodgson, 1993) commonly distinguishes two kinds of learning:
- single-loop learning concerned with obtaining knowledge to solve specific problems based on existing premises;
- double-loop learning concerned with establishing new premises such as mental models and perspectives (Argyris and Schön, 1974; 1978; Bateson, 1973; Kieras and Bovair, 1984).

Nonaka and Takeuchi (1995, p. 45) criticised organisational learning theories for failing to recognise knowledge development as learning. The metaphor of individual learning is still widely used and what constitutes organisational learning inadequately defined (Weick, 1991). The concept of knowledge creation is underdeveloped in organisational learning models which assume that some artificial intervention is required to set up double-loop learning.

Garvin (1993) distinguishes between cognitive learning, related to the understanding and use of new concepts, and behavioural learning, related in the physical ability to act, and identifies three stages in the learning process. During the initial stage, cognitive learning leads to the alteration and improvement of thought patterns and knowledge base. These are translated into new work practices, in the subsequent behavioural learning stage. During the third stage, the actions which follow cognitive and behavioural learning lead to visible performance improvements for the organisation. Although such rational analyses of organisational learning are appealing they fail to recognise the importance of interactions between cognitive and behavioural learning (Kim, 1993) and fail to elaborate the mechanisms by which individual learning becomes organisational learning (Senge, 1990).

More widely accepted cyclical models of learning illustrate the links between the two types of learning. Kim's (1993) analysis in addition incorporates the learning function of active memory, pivotal to the transfer from individual to organisational learning, referring to conceptual and operational learning (instead of cognitive and behavioural learning). Conceptual learning occurs through assessment and design; the ensuing implementation and observation correspond to operational learning. The conceptual-operational learning cycle

Figure 2: **Integrated model of individual learning**

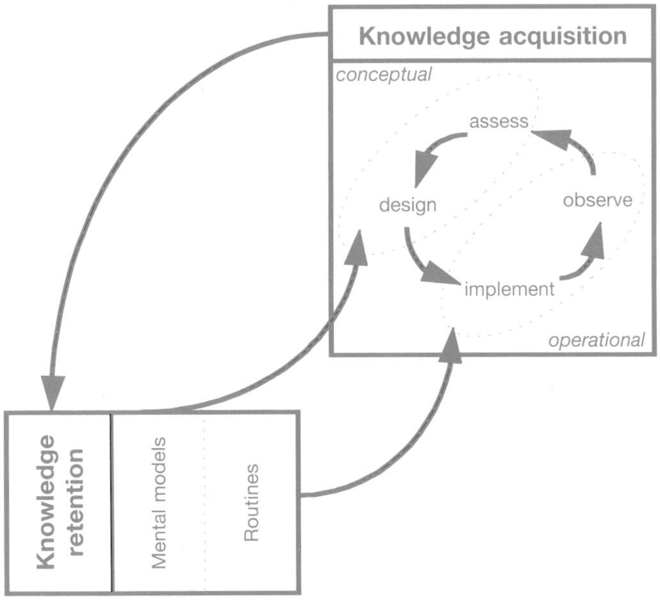

Adapted from kim (1993)

describes the knowledge acquisition process. It is not built around a linear cause and effect relationship, but on the interaction between the two types of learning. Indeed in some cases, conceptual learning may lead to operational learning and in others the reverse may be true.

Knowledge retention and the role of active memory are equally important because they determine the individual and organisational outcomes of the learning process. Active memory refers to 'the active structures that affect our thinking process and the actions we take' (Kim, 1993). They comprise what are described as mental models elsewhere in the literature (Senge, 1990). Individual mental models act as filters shaping our understanding of reality; they evolve as conceptual learning takes place. The other aspect of active memory is developing routines through operational learning. Figure 1 illustrates this learning process according to Kim, highlighting the interactions between conceptual and operational learning and demonstrating how they respectively contribute to, and are influenced by, the formation of mental models and routines.

4.3. Underlying intellectual abilities

In considering the development of KSCs by individuals, not only are learning processes important but also underlying intellectual abilities (Ackerman, 1987; 1988; 1992). Intellectual abilities are evidently important prerequisites for acquiring KSCs but intelligence cannot be taken as a proxy for KSCs even if it is a reasonable predictor of ability to acquire these attributes. Also, measuring intelligence is complex and needs to be more sophisticated than the IQ measures that are not free from cultural bias.

General cognitive ability is the focus of psychometric models of human intelligence, information processing models and Piaget's (1947) model of cognitive structural development. According to the psychometric approach, intelligence relates to abilities and aptitudes that are independent of content (as in knowledge) and context (Carroll, 1993). It underpins purposeful action, reasoning, effective learning and meaningful interaction with the environment. According to information-processing approaches, intelligence is analogous to a machine with general system features such as processing speed, working memory capacity, processing capacity, which enables the individual to acquire specific knowledge and skills. Piaget also assumed general cognitive competence but attributed a major role to processes of adaptation by which an individual passes through a sequence of developmental stages leading to increasingly flexible and abstract knowledge and action competencies. Specialised cognitive competencies are prerequisites for superior performance in a particular activity, whether defined narrowly (e.g. solving second order differential equations) or broadly (e.g. analytical competence).

Carroll's (1993) hierarchical three stratum-theory of intelligence, starting with general intelligence at the primary level, is quite comprehensive. There are eight, second-order-influences, (fluid intelligence, crystallised intelligence, memory and learning, visual perception, acoustic perception, originality and fluency of ideas, speed of information processing and mental speed) and finally 68 third-order sub-constructs incorporating virtually all psychometrically-defined abilities distinguished in earlier work. According to some authorities it is practical intelligence (Sternberg and Wagner, 1986; Sternberg and Kaufman, 1998), intellectual attributes amenable to ready application that matters, while others have argued that social intelligence (Keating, 1978), cultural intelligence (Earley and Ang, 2003) and emotional intelligence (Goleman, 1995) are essential in a work context. However these are less amenable to evaluation and more controversial than traditional psychometric measures on which Caroll's constructs are based.

4.4. Knowledge

Knowledge is sometimes viewed as if it was a concrete manifestation of abstract intelligence, but it is actually the result of an interaction between intelligence (capacity to learn) and situation (opportunity to learn), so is more socially-constructed than intelligence. Knowledge includes theory and concepts and tacit knowledge gained as a result of the experience of performing certain tasks. Understanding refers to more holistic knowledge of processes and contexts and may be distinguished as know-why, as opposed know-that.

A distinction is often made between general knowledge, which is essential irrespective of any occupational context or so fundamental as to be considered basic life knowledge, and knowledge that is specific to a sector or particular group of occupations and only likely to be encountered in such context. Weinert (1999, p. 24), for example, distinguishes:

> general world knowledge (generally measured by vocabulary tests that are part of many intelligence measurements, and overlapping considerably with what is defined as crystallised intelligence), and more arbitrary specialised knowledge. This specialised knowledge is necessary for meeting content specific demands and solving content-specific tasks. In contrast to general intellectual abilities, one can consider arbitrary knowledge as a demand-specific competence.

Collin (1997, p. 297) cites Gardner's association of know-how with tacit knowledge and know-that with propositional knowledge. Another way of expressing this distinction is between declarative knowledge (knowing what), and procedural knowledge (knowing how). From this perspective, it is often argued that acquiring declarative knowledge (explicit factual knowledge) must precede developing procedural knowledge, which relates to utilising knowledge in context. Gagne's (1962) model of hierarchical knowledge fits with this approach, identifying the knowledge set necessary for understanding, learning and performing well on a criterion task. This is then traced back to each subordinate set of psychological knowledge, providing a description of knowledge that is increasingly elementary and general.

Each knowledge and learning hierarchy therefore rests on primary mental abilities, with the implicit assumption of a general learning transfer capacity and logic of knowledge acquisition. In all domains there is some logic that acquiring and comprehending new knowledge demands facilitating cognitive prerequisites and specific knowledge and skills. Given this interaction between knowledge and skills, their separation in a typology is not easy. Indeed, for Klieme et al. (2004, p. 70), higher competency levels are characterised by the increasing proceduralisation of knowledge, so 'at higher levels, knowledge is converted to skills'.

4.5. Skill

Skill was characterised by Pear (1927) as being concerned with the quantity and quality of motor output: 'skill is the integration of well-adjusted muscular performances' (Pear, 1948, p. 92). While for Pear the emphasis was on manual, motor skills, his contemporary Hans Renold in 1928 defined skill as 'any combination, useful to industry, of mental and physical qualities which require considerable training to acquire' (More, 1980, p. 15). While Renold was therefore introducing a cognitive dimension alongside the manual, his emphasis on training ignores the fact the skills may equally be acquired through practice, without training. Usually the term skill is used to refer to a level of performance, in the sense of accuracy and speed in performing particular tasks (skilled performance). Skilled performance has long been a subject of psychological enquiry and is of obvious interest to employers. Bryan and Harter (1897; 1899), who undertook one of the earliest systematic studies of (practical) skills acquired in the work environment (by telegraph operators at Western Union), demonstrated that skill acquisition involves a series of stages associated with reaching plateaux of performance and that improvements continue well beyond achieving an adequate level. Swift (1904) adopted a similar approach in researching skill among typists and later also telegraphers (Swift, 1910). Motor skill acquisition has continued to occupy the attention of researchers, increasing understanding of the role of perception, feedback and other factors (Newell, 1991; Schmidt, 1975; 1988).

The classic learning curves apparent in this early work of Bryan and Harter are a recurrent feature of skills research. In Cox's (1934) study of manual skill, which was not defined but involved both physical psychomotor abilities and mental cognitive abilities, performance in terms of speed and accuracy was measured in experiments with repetitive assembly operations. Parallel learning curves were apparent for subjects developing proficiency through practice and for those who also received training; the performance of the latter group was higher than among those not receiving training. Cox (1934, p. 238-239) argued that the relatively short initial phase of deep slope in the practice curves was associated with the cognitive aspects of manual operations, while the longer more gradual descent was associated with the motor aspects. Subsequent studies demonstrated that plateaux and regressions do not always occur and when they do there is no justification in associating them with particular types or stages of learning (Fuchs, 1962; Keller, 1958). The early finding that diminishing marginal improvement in performance appears to continue indefinitely has generally been confirmed in later research, which led to the conclusion that learning can be described as a linear function of the logarithms of times and trials (Crossman, 1959; Snoddy, 1926) and ultimately to the power law of practice (Newell and Rosenbloom, 1981).

Another strand of skills research has concerned transfer of training, particularly the extent to which proficiency and experience in one task helps performance in another. In general, transfer of motor skills has only been found to occur where the tasks have particular elements in common, undermining the argument for developing general abilities that will improve performance in various activities (Adams, 1987; Gagné, Foster and Crowley, 1948). This observation has been shown to apply equally to the transfer of cognitive skill (Singley and Anderson, 1989). One conclusion of Cox's studies was that 'skill developed by the mere repetition of one manual operation confers little advantage in the performance of other operations that may be subsequently undertaken' (Cox, 1934, p. 176).

Welford (1968, p. 12-13), who defined skill as a combination of factors resulting in 'competent, expert, rapid and accurate performance', regarded this as equally applicable to manual operations and mental activities. Welford's (1968; 1976) work focused on perceptual-motor performance, as has much of skills research since the two are intimately linked in practice (Fuchs, 1962; Lintern and Gopher, 1978). Welford's work shows how actions are selected and coordinated at different levels of skilled performance and the conditions of practice and training that promote the acquisition and transfer of skill. More recently, research into skilled performance has increasingly taken into account broader cognitive skills such as problem solving and decision making. This demonstrates the difficulty in regarding such cognitive competences as knowledge rather than skill. Indeed, there is substantial evidence that acquiring skill and demonstrating skilled performance involve a combination of underlying perceptual, cognitive and motor skills (Carlson and Yaure, 1990; Salthouse, 1986). Also, retaining even relatively simple motor skills appears to depend upon understanding of results (Lavery, 1962) and verbalised knowledge (Berry and Broadbent, 1984), or knowledge that is articulated in the course of developing such skills. Moreover, knowledge and working memory play a major role in acquiring skills (Chase and Ericsson, 1982) including procedural skills (Carlson, Sullivan and Schneider, 1989), problem-solving skills (Carlson et al., 1990) and complex cognitive skills (Logie et al., 1989; McKeithen et al., 1981).

Fitts and colleagues (Fitts et al., 1961; Fitts and Posner, 1967) developed a three stage framework for skill acquisition: (i) the cognitive phase of understanding the nature of the task how it should be performed involves conscious cognitive processes; (ii) the associative phase involves inputs linked more directly to appropriate actions and reduced interference from outside demands and finally (iii) the autonomous phase occurs when actions are automatic requiring no conscious control (see Garvin's three-stage model of learning above). Based on this approach, Anderson (1981; 1982; 1983; 1987) developed a framework for acquiring cognitive skill in which the declarative and procedural phases correspond with Fitt's cognitive and autonomous phases. In place of an intermediary associative phase, Anderson argued there is a continuous process of 'knowledge compilation' involving the conversion of declarative knowledge into procedural knowledge. Rasmussen (1983; 1986) proposed a further framework relating to skilled performance, distinguishing knowledge-based performance (see Fitts's cognitive phase), rule-based performance (which also involves conscious control, but based on stored rules) and skill-based performance (see Fitts's autonomous phase).

Proctor and Dutta (1995, p. 18) in what is arguably the most authoritative text on skill acquisition and performance, define skill as 'goal-directed, well-organised behaviour that is acquired through practice and performed with economy of effort'. Each element of the definition is important: first, skill develops over time, with practice; second, it is goal-directed in response to some demand in the external environment; third, it is acquired when components of behaviour are structured into coherent patterns; and finally, cognitive demands are reduced as skill develops. Inevitably, to measure skill, most researchers use speed and/ or accuracy of performance, two variables between which there is inevitably a degree of trade-off. In further articulating their conception of skill, Proctor and Dutta (1995) distinguish perceptual skills, response selection skills, motor skills and problem-solving skills. Perceptual skills are concerned with the ability to make distinctions and judgements; more complex situations require attentional control for processing but many tasks that initially require attention become automatised. Skill in selecting the appropriate response can be developed with practice; reaction time is affected by the number of alternatives and can be accelerated by providing advance information, thereby reducing the alternatives. Motor skills are the manual aspects of performance such as speed and accuracy of physical movements or dexterity. Problem-solving skills, while dependent upon intellect and mental models, can be acquired and developed through practice.

4.6. Competence

There is such confusion and debate about the concept of competence that it is impossible to identify or impute a coherent theory or to arrive at a definition capable of accommodating and reconciling all the different ways the term is used (Elleström, 1997; Robotham and Jubb, 1996). This terminological confusion often reflects conflation of distinct concepts and inconsistent use of terms as much as different cultural traditions. However, some differences are attributable to different epistemological assumptions (Pate, Martin and Robertson, 2003) and the rationale for the use of competence often determines the definition (Hoffman, 1999). As Norris (1991, p. 332) argued, 'as tacit understandings of the word [competence] have been overtaken by the need to define precisely and [to] operationalise concepts, the practical has become shrouded in theoretical confusion and the apparently simple has become profoundly complicated'. Describing competence as a 'fuzzy concept', Boon and van der Klink (2002, p. 6) none the less acknowledge it as a 'useful term, bridging the gap between education and job requirements'.

Different cultural contexts influence the understanding of competence (Cseh, 2003) and this is especially important in relation to the extent to which competence is defined by cultural literacy involving group identities such as race, gender, age and class (ascription), as opposed to demonstrable behaviour (achievement). As Jeris and Johnson (2004, p. 1104) note, the distinction is confounded by the role of ascription in providing access to education and career opportunities that enable achievement: 'As much as the behavioural and skill-based performance assessments portend to be 'neutral and objective,' the ascriptive elements remain present and troubling for today's increasingly diverse workplaces'. There have been few attempts (notably Boon and van der Klink, 2002 in the US, Eraut, 1994 in the UK) to situate competence in terms of sociocultural practices, which as Jeris and Johnson (2004, p. 1108) note:

is disturbing in light of the strong bonds between identifying competencies and tying them to practice standards. These standards, once developed, find their way into practice through certification of people and processes, through accrediting agencies (public and private) for all sorts of educational programs, and through qualification examinations and licensure requirements. … The commodification of competence into certifiable competencies privileges the KSA (knowledge, skills and attitudes) worldview, and turns what Boon and van der Klink (2002) found to be a somewhat flexible concept into a rigid sorting mechanism that may have grave consequences for marginalised groups.

Snyder and Ebeling (1992) refer to competence in a functional sense, but use 'competencies' in the plural. Some authors consistently use 'competency' when referring to occupational competence (Boam and Sparrow, 1992; Hendry, Arthur and Jones, 1995; Mitrani, Dalziel and Fitt, 1992; Smith, 1993) or treat the two as synonymous (Brown, 1993; 1994; McBeath, 1990). Dale and Iles (1992) distinguish occupational skills from psycho-social characteristics, but use competence and competency to describe both in discussing their role in assessing managerial skills. Hartle (1995, p. 107) argues that competency as 'a characteristic of an individual that has been shown to drive superior job performance includes both visible competencies of knowledge and skills and underlying elements of competencies, like traits and motives'. Elkin (1990) associates competences with micro-level job performance and competencies with higher management attributes and, in defining 'managerial competencies for the future', Cockerill (1989) combines output competences, like effective presentation skills, with input competencies such as self-confidence.

The difficulty of using competence as an overarching term as well as a specific one is demonstrated by the tautological definition provided by Dooley et al. (2004, p. 317): 'Competency-based behavioural anchors are defined as performance capabilities needed to demonstrate knowledge, skill and ability (competency) acquisition'. According to this construction, competency is a sub-set of itself.

The few attempts to establish coherent terminology (Boak, 1991; Tate, 1995b; Winterton and Winterton, 1999; Woodruffe, 1991) have had little impact to date. Boak (1991) argues that 'competency', in the American sense, complements competence, as used in the UK occupational standards. Burgoyne (1988a) similarly distinguishes 'being competent' (meeting the job demands) from 'having competencies' (possessing the necessary attributes to perform competently). Woodruffe (1991) offers the clearest statement, contrasting areas of competence, defined as aspects of the job which an individual can perform, with competency referring to a person's behaviour and underpinning competent performance. Woodruffe's definition is endorsed by Tate (1995b, p. 86) who warns against confusing input competencies with output competences.

Mangham (1986) noted that competence may relate to personal models, outcome models or education and training models, as well as to the standards approach in which benchmarking criteria are used. Mansfield (2004, p. 304) similarly contrasts three different uses of competence: outcomes (vocational standards describing what people need to be able to do in employment); tasks that people do (describing what currently happens); and personal traits or characteristics (describing what people are like). Weinert (1999, p. 7) lists nine different ways in which competence has been defined or interpreted: general cognitive ability; specialised cognitive skills; competence-performance model; modified competence-performance model; objective and subjective self-concepts; motivated action tendencies; action competence; key competencies; meta-competencies.

White (1959) is credited with having introduced the term competence to describe those personality characteristics associated with superior performance and high motivation. Postulating a relationship between cognitive competence and motivational action tendencies, White defined competence as an 'effective interaction (of the individual) with the environment' and arguing there is a competence motivation in addition to competence as achieved capacity. Theory building in this area has argued that an individual's system of knowledge and beliefs, formed through experience with their own competence and achievement, influences subsequent performance through expectations, attitudes and interpretation.

McClelland (1973) followed this approach and developed tests to predict competence as opposed intelligence, but subsequently (McClelland, 1976) also described this characteristic underlying superior performance as 'competency', introducing the approach to the consulting firm that became Hay McBer. Measures of competence were developed as an alternative to using traditional tests of cognitive intelligence because these were held to be poor predictors of job performance (Pottinger and Goldsmith, 1979), although Barrett and Dipenet (1991) defended the predictive power of intelligence tests. The competence approach starts from the opposite end, observing successful and effective job performers to determine how these individuals differ from less successful performers. Competency captures skills and dispositions beyond cognitive ability such as self-awareness, self-regulation and social skills; while some of these may also be found in personality taxonomies (Barrick and Mount, 1991) competencies are fundamentally behavioural and susceptible to learning (McClelland, 1998). This tradition has remained particularly influential in the US, with competency defined in terms of underlying characteristics of people that are causally related to effective or superior performance in a job, generalising across situations and enduring for a reasonably long period of time (Boyatzis, 1982; Guion, 1991; Hay Group et al., 1996; Klemp and Spencer, 1982; Spencer and Spencer, 1993).

The roots of the competence-performance approach are in the work of Chomsky (1980), who described linguistic competence as a universal, inherited, modularised ability to acquire the mother tongue, as distinct from performance (ability to understand and use the language). Chomsky's model of linguistic competence and performance has influenced similar models of numerical competence, spatial competence and other areas of domain-specific knowledge. Overton (1985) modified the competence-performance model by introducing moderating variables such as cognitive style, memory capacity, familiarity with the task situation, and other individual difference variables. Developmental psychologists (e.g. Gelman and Greeno, 1989; Greeno, Riley and Gelman, 1984; Sophian, 1997) commonly break competence down into three analytically distinct components:

(a) conceptual competence, rule-based, abstract knowledge about an entire domain;
(b) procedural competence, procedures and skills needed to apply conceptual competence in concrete situations;
(c) performance competencies, required to assess a problem and select a suitable strategy for its solution.

This approach has been criticised for its limitation to cognitive aspects and neglect of socially-transmitted, subjective perspectives of the individual (Elbers, 1991). Also, it appears to be unidirectional, considering the influences of competence on performance (behaviour), while neglecting the shaping of competence through performance (Sophian, 1997), when it is clear that developing competence depends upon the learning and practice opportunities available and taken (Ericsson, Krampe and Tesch-Römer, 1993).

A distinction can be made between objective competence (performance and potential performance measured with standard tests) and subjective competence (assessment of abilities and skills needed to master tasks and solve problems relevant to performance) (Sternberg and Kolligian, 1990). Stäudel (1987) further divides subjective competence into three components:

(a) heuristic competence (generalised expectancy system concerning the effectiveness of one's abilities across different situations – generalised self concept);
(b) epistemological competence (beliefs and confidence that one possesses domain- specific skills and knowledge to master tasks and problems within a specific content domain – domain specific self-concept);
(c) actualised competence (momentary subjective self-confidence that one possesses the abilities, knowledge and skills believed necessary for success in a concrete learning or performance situation).

Action competence includes all the cognitive, motivational and social prerequisites for successful learning and application and has been used to analyse the conditions for success in meeting task goals. Models typically include:

(a) general problem-solving competence,
(b) critical thinking skills,
(c) domain-general and domain-specific knowledge,
(d) realistic, positive self confidence,
(e) social competences.

Action competence as used by Boyatzis (1982) in defining management competence, includes intellectual abilities, content-specific knowledge, cognitive skills, domain-specific strategies, routines and sub-routines, motivational tendencies, volitional control systems, personal value orientations, and social behaviours into a complex system that specifies what is needed to meet the demands of a particular role (Lévy-Leboyer, 1996). In addition to cognitive and motivational components, these models include other skills such as specific and non-specific vocational competencies and institution-specific competencies. Competence in this sense has less to do with the psychological prerequisites for successful individual action and more with the individual, role-specific and collective conditions underlying successful performance in institutions and social groups. From this perspective, what matters is that there is a social network of competencies that allows optimal use of resources for achieving the goals of the institution. This approach underlies the current focus on developing institution-specific competences (Foss and Knudsen, 1996).

Key competences are context-independent, applicable and effective across different institutional settings, occupations and tasks. These typically include basal competences, such as literacy, numeracy, general education; methodological competences, like problem solving, IT skills; communication skills, including writing and presentation skills; and judgement competences, such as critical thinking.

Meta-competence is concerned with an individual's knowledge of their own intellectual strengths and weaknesses, how to apply skills and knowledge in various task situations and how to acquire missing competences (Nelson and Narens, 1990). These include skills in planning, initiating, monitoring and evaluating one's own cognitive processes; experience and knowledge about different task difficulties; knowledge about learning and problem solving; skills in using effective cognitive aids and tools, such as graphics and analogies. Often also described as generic and overarching, (Reynolds and Snell, 1988), meta-competences typically include 'learning to learn' (Nuthall, 1999; Nyhan, 1991) and 'coping with uncertainty' (Brown, 1994). Drawing on the work of Burgoyne (1989b) and Kanugo and Misra (1992), Brown (1993, p. 32) defines meta-competences as 'higher-order abilities which have to do with being able to learn, adapt, anticipate and create, rather than with being able to demonstrate that one has the ability to do'. The common theme with such lists of meta-competencies is they relate to the cognitive aspects of work, especially with the processes of learning and reflection that are critical to developing new mental models (Burgoyne and Stewart, 1976; Hyland, 1992; Kolb et al., 1986; Linstead, 1991; Nordhaug, 1993).

In summary, if intellectual capabilities are needed to develop knowledge and operationalising knowledge is part of developing skills, all are prerequisites to developing competence, together with other social and attitudinal aspects. Weinert (2001, p. 29), for example, lists a range of dimensions held to influence an individual's degree of competence:

(a) ability,
(b) knowledge,
(c) understanding,
(d) skill,
(e) action,
(f) experience,
(g) motivation.

It is important to note these are issues affecting the development of competence, not dimensions of competence. While motivation, for example, has been included as an aspect of competence in some writings, we argue below that it is important to maintain the distinction because someone may be competent and not motivated or motivated and not competent.

5. Use of typologies of KSCs

Having considered some of the concepts underpinning of KSCs, this section explores recent developments in the use of typologies of KSCs and some of the problems in relation to generic KSCs, alternative interpretative approaches, notions of expertise and higher order work, and measurement and assessment issues.

5.1. Generic KSC typologies

The first and most influential generic typology of KSCs was developed by Bloom and colleagues from the 1960s (Bloom, 1976; Bloom, Hastings and Madaus, 1971; Bloom, Mesia and Krathwohl, 1964) for use in educational establishments. Generally known as Bloom's taxonomy, it is based on three domains of educational activities: cognitive, affective, and psychomotor (which was added later). The cognitive domain relates to mental skills (knowledge), the affective domain for growth in feelings or emotional areas (attitudes), while the psychomotor domain is concerned with manual or physical skills (skills). This taxonomy is influential in the training world and trainers frequently refer to these as KSA (knowledge, skills and attitudes). This taxonomy relates to learning outcomes, since it defines what, after the training process, individuals should have acquired in terms of knowledge, skills or attitudes. The categories in each domain can be thought of as degrees of difficulty, so each must be mastered before the next can be developed and they are therefore analogous to the vertical dimension or reference levels. Bloom's taxonomy has strongly influenced the development of the Irish qualifications framework (see below).

The cognitive domain involves knowledge and developing intellectual skills. This includes recalling or recognising specific facts, procedural patterns, and concepts that serve in developing intellectual abilities and skills. There are six major categories, starting from the simplest behaviour to the most complex: knowledge (recall of data); comprehension (understand meaning, interpret); application (use a concept in a new situation); analysis (separate material into component parts); synthesis (build a structure or pattern); and evaluation (make judgements). The affective domain includes the manner in which we deal with things emotionally, such as feelings, values, appreciation, enthusiasms, motivations and attitudes. The five major categories in order of difficulty are: receiving phenomena (awareness and attention); responding to phenomena (active participation); valuing (acceptance and commitment); organisation (organising values into priorities); and internalising values (having a value system that controls behaviour). The psychomotor domain includes physical movement, coordination, and use of the motor-skill areas. Developing these skills requires practice and is measured in terms of speed, precision, distance, procedures or techniques in execution. Bloom's original work did not elaborate the competences in the psychomotor domain, but Simpson (1972) proposed the following seven major categories: perception (using sensory cues to guide motor activity); set (readiness to act); guided response (imitation, trial and error); mechanism (intermediate stage in learning a complex skill); complex overt response (skilful performance of motor acts that involve complex movement patterns); adaptation (modify movement patterns to meet special requirements); and origination (developing new movement patterns to fit specific problem).

The use of generic KSC typologies and frameworks in enterprises, as opposed to in education, has been promoted by efforts to link development to organisational strategy and to retain core competence as a key source of competitive advantage (McClelland, 1994; Shröder, 1989). There is an apparent paradox in this, since if concentrating on core competences that are 'distinctive and specific to each individual organisation' is what gives competitive advantage (Barnett, 1994; Bergenhenegouwen, ten Horn and Mooijman, 1996), the scope for generic frameworks is limited (Lindsay and Stuart, 1997; Thompson, Stuart and Lindsay, 1996).

The generic approach is concerned with developing highly transferable generic skills and competences that are required for most jobs and distinctive from more workplace-specific technical knowledge and skills (Stasz, 1997). The State Commission on achieving necessary skills (SCANS) established by the US Secretary of Labor, included in this category foundation skills (reading, writing and arithmetic); thinking skills (reasoning, problem-solving); personal qualities (responsibility, self-esteem); and work competencies (resources, interpersonal, information, systems and technology) (SCANS, 1992). A similar initiative in Australia identified seven key competences (collecting, analysing and organising information; expressing ideas and information; planning and organising activities; working with others and in teams; using mathematical ideas and techniques; solving problems; and using technology) which were assumed to be transferable from education to the world of work (Mayer, 1992).

Strategies emphasising core competence as a key organisational resource that can be exploited to gain competitive advantage are prevalent in the management literature of the 1990s (Barney, 1995; Campbell and Sommers Luchs, 1997; Hussey, 1988; 1996; Mitrani, Dalziel and Fitt, 1992; Nadler and Tushman, 1999; Quinn, Anderson and Finkelstein, 1996; Thurbin, 1995; Tobin, 1993). Hamel and Prahalad (1994) argued that it is necessary to identify the core competence of an organisation, defined as 'the collective learning in the organisation, especially how to coordinate diverse production skills and integrate multiple streams of technologies' (Prahalad and Hamel, 1990, p. 82). The key to competitive advantage lies in the capacity within the organisation for developing and maintaining core competence.

The virtue of the core competence approach is that it 'recognises the complex interaction of people, skills and technologies that drives firm performance and addresses the importance of learning and path dependency in its evolution' (Scarborough, 1998, p. 229). Competency modelling is about identifying the critical success factors driving performance in organisations (Lucia and Lepsinger, 1999) and competence assessment is concerned with determining the extent to which individuals have these critical competencies (Spencer, McClelland and Kelner, 1997). Teece, Pisano and Schuen (1991, p. 20) developed the concept of dynamic capabilities; or 'the ability of an organisation to learn, adapt, change, and renew over time'. All these approaches depend upon organisational meta-learning processes, where learning and renewal is emphasised at the organisational level (Lei, Hitt and Bettis, 1996).

Since the end of the 1990s, competency-based HRM has become widespread in the US, in relation to HRD in general, leadership, selection, retention and remuneration (Allbredge and Nilan, 2000; Athey and Orth, 1999; Dubois and Rothwell, 2004; Foxan, 1998; Harvey, Speier and Novicevic, 2000; Naquin and Holton, 2002; Rodriguez et al., 2002). In this renaissance, competency has a much broader conception than hitherto, including knowledge and skills alongside the behavioural or psycho-social characteristics in the McClelland tradition. Even within the predominantly behavioural approach, many conceptions of competency now include knowledge and skills alongside attitudes, behaviours, work habits, abilities and personal characteristics (Gangani, McLean and Braden, 2004; Green, 1999; Lucia and Lepsinger, 1999; Mirabile, 1997; Naquin and Wilson, 2002; Nitardy and McLean, 2002; Russ-Eft, 1995).

Much of the recent US literature focuses on job-related (functional) competences (Aragon and Johnson, 2002; Boon and van der Klink, 2002; Klemp, 1980; O'Neil, 1997; Piskurich and Saunders, 1998), often with associated fundamental behavioural competencies. For example, in the influential leadership competency model developed by Holton and Lynham (2000), six 'competency domains are identified relating to performance at the organisation, process and individual levels. These domains are broken down into 'competency groups and then further divided into sub-competencies. At the organisation performance level, the two competency domains identified are strategic thinking and strategic stewardship, beneath which there are, respectively, four and five competency groups, with further sub-competencies (Collins, Lowe and Arnett, 2000). Similarly, at the process level, the two competency domains identified are process management and process planning, each broken down into three competency groups, with further sub-competencies (Baker, Walsh and Marjerison, 2000). At the individual level, the two competency domains, employee performance and employee appraisal, are each subdivided into four competency groups, with further sub-competencies (Wilson, Boudreaux and Edwards, 2000). All of the competencies listed are based on functional job-related standards, rather than behavioural competencies (although some are clearly underpinned by behavioural competencies). While the behavioural competency approach is still much in evidence in the US, a broader conception of competence, including job-related functional skills and basic knowledge, is clearly gaining ground.

5.2. Interpretative approaches

The idea that generic KSCs are transferable across different knowledge domains has been widely questioned (Billet, 2000; Perkins and Salomon, 1989). Collin (1989) argued it is futile attempting to capture management skills and competences in a mechanistic, reductionist fashion, while Jacobs (1989) believed the use of generic competences led to neglect of soft skills that are expected to be of increasing importance in the future. Thorpe and Holman (1997) similarly concluded that 'the methodology of MCI [Management Charter Initiative, which designed the occupational standards for managers in the United Kingdom] has caused it to overlook ot inadequately address factors thought to be important in managing which are difficult to describe or reduce to behavioural terminology'. By contrast, Otter (1994) claimed the competence-based approach in the United Kingdom presents problems for management since NVQs are constructed in terms of competence within a specific occupational context, whereas managerial competences are generic rather than occupationally specific. Otter is confusing sector with occupation; managers as an occupational group, like electricians, are found in a range of sectors and it is the occupation, rather than the sector which is the focus of competence and occupational standards.

Spencer and Spencer (1993) demonstrated the use of the McClelland/McBer job competence assessment (JCA) methodology with an analysis of 650 jobs to propose generic job models. For them, 'competencies' include:

> motives, traits, self-concepts, attitudes or values, content knowledge or cognitive or behavioural skills - any individual characteristic that can be measured or counted reliably and that can be shown to differentiate significantly between superior and average performers or between effective and ineffective performers (Spencer and Spencer, 1993, p. 4).

Stasz (1997) found that employers identified key elements of the SCANS competences as essential for work performance but argued these were common rather than generic, the point being the competences needed to be embedded in particular contexts to be understood (Stuart and Lindsay, 1997). Therefore, while there are common competences, these are displayed differently in different work situations and can only be understood in particular contexts. Since most definitions of KSCs are centred on the individual, these are viewed as independent of the social and task-specific context in which performance occurs, yet 'skill level is a characteristic not only of a person but also of a context. People do not have competences independent of context'. (Fischer et al., 1993, p. 113). Hence Stoof et al. (2002) and Sandberg (2000) adopt a constructivist approach to defining competence, arguing that it is governed by the context in which it is applied.

Identifying competence is generally centred on job analysis, but this is essentially a rationalist approach derived from scientific management. Taylor (1911, p. 6), for all the limitations of the principles of work organisation he was promoting, nevertheless argued that organisations were all seeking better, more competent employees at all levels and that this implied a responsibility to train. While Taylorism involved an intense division of labour and reduction of work tasks to simple elements, it also entailed identifying workers' competences and the routines associated with effective deployment to develop these more widely and improve overall performance.

Sandberg (1994) distinguishes three approaches within this rationalist tradition: worker-oriented; work-oriented; and multimethod-oriented. The worker-oriented approach defines competence in terms of 'attributes possessed by workers, typically represented as knowledge, skills, abilities (KSA) [2] and personal traits needed for effective work performance' (Sandberg, 2000, p. 49). The component attributes may be identified through investigation with job incumbents and supervisors, then rated to establish quantitative measures of the attributes that may be correlated with performance measures. This is essentially the approach of assessment centres (Woodruffe, 1990) that seek to identify job competency as 'an underlying characteristic of a person in that it may be a motive, trait, skill, aspect of one's self-image or social role or a body of knowledge he or she uses' (Boyatzis, 1982, p. 21). Since this notion of competence is one of an individual underlying characteristic, it is inevitably regarded as generic and context-independent. Work-process oriented approaches, however, take work as the starting point, identify work activities that are central to a particular job role and then identify the personal attributes

---

[2] KSA normally refers in the training literature to Knowledge, skills and attitudes, which approximates closely to the way in which the TWG has used KSC and is consistent with Bloom's taxonomy.

needed to achieve appropriate outcomes. This is the approach most often adopted in considering strategic or distinctive firm competences underpinning competitive advantage (Henderson and Cockburn, 1994; Prahalad and Hamel, 1990; Snow and Hrebiniak, 1980). Sandberg argues that multimethod-oriented approaches, which involve aligning personal attributes with work activities, are more adequate for a comprehensive analysis.

Sandberg (2000, p. 48-49) criticises the rationalist approach because:

> human competence is described as being constituted by a specific set of attributes such as knowledge and skills, which workers use to accomplish their work. Further, attributes are seen as context-independent. That is, a specific attribute such as communication skills is regarded as having a fixed meaning in itself; it is independent of context and can thus be adopted in a range of work activities. This view of competence originates in a dualist ontology and objectivist epistemology underlying the rationalistic research tradition. Dualist ontology underlies a division of the phenomenon of competence into two separate entities, namely the worker and the work. The objectivist epistemology, in this instance referring to an objective, knowable work beyond the worker, has led to descriptions of work activities that are independent of the workers who accomplish them.

The rationalist approach of operationalising attributes into quantitative measures has equally been criticised for creating abstract, overly narrow and simplified descriptions of competence that fail adequately to reflect the complexity of competence in work performance (Attewell, 1990; Norris, 1991; Sandberg, 1994). In place of the rationalistic methods, interpretative approaches, derived from phenomenology, are proposed which do not see competence as a duality but 'worker and work form one entity through lived experience of work' (Sandberg, 2000, p. 50) so competence is constituted by the meaning the work has for the worker in their experience (Dall'Alba and Sandberg, 1996).

Dreyfus and Dreyfus (1986), who used an interpretative approach to investigate competence among pilots and others, found that attributes used in accomplishing work are bound to the work context regardless of the competence attained and that in the work situation individuals acquire situational or context-dependent knowledge and skills. Other interpretative studies, with nurses (Benner, 1984) and police officers (Fielding, 1988a; 1988b), have equally demonstrated that attributes acquire context-dependency through individuals' experience of work. One of the advantages of the interpretative approach is in acknowledging workers' tacit knowledge and skills (Polanyi, 1967), which can be overlooked if competence is treated as context-free since the way people work in practice seldom accords with the formal job description. Tacit competences, including those of so-called unskilled workers (Kusterer, 1978), can have a determining impact on the success of an enterprise (Flanagan, McGinn and Thornhill, 1993).

Using an interpretative approach with engine designers in a car company, Sandberg (1994) also found that:

> human competence is not primarily constituted by a specific set of attributes. Instead, workers' knowledge, skills and other attributes used in accomplishing the work are preceded by and based upon the workers' understanding of work. … The way of understanding a particular work delimit certain attributes (such as knowledge and skills) as essential and organises them into a distinctive form of competence in performing that work (Sandberg, 2000, p. 54).

Sandberg argues that since an individual's performance is influenced by their interaction with others in the workplace, it is collective rather than individual competence that should be the focus. In defining collective competence, Sjöstrand (1979) distinguished between 'competence mass', the organisation's entire resource base, and 'distinctive competence', those activities the organisation is able to perform more effectively than competitors. Hitt and Ireland (1985; 1986) adopted a similar approach in relating distinctive competence to firm performance. From a cognitive perspective, Leonard-Barton (1992) defines collective competence as a four-dimensional knowledge system incorporating: knowledge and skills of the employees; that embedded in technical systems; that created and controlled by formal and informal managerial systems; and the values and norms assigned to particular knowledge and skills.

As with individual competence, from this rationalistic perspective, collective competence is defined in such a way the organisation is separated from its task and work from the collective, so we are 'unable to take into account the ways in which the members of the collective experience, and make sense of, their work' (Sandberg, 2000, p. 57). Offering an alternative interpretative perspective, Sandberg (2000, p. 59) stresses the importance of shared understanding and common culture underpinning how individuals interact to define collective competence: 'a system of shared symbols that denote the central meaning aspects of the collective's work experience'. The implication of the interpretative, cultural perspective on competence is that development of particular knowledge and skills always takes place within a specific understanding of work so that competence development should not focus on transferring knowledge and skills to individuals but on changing workers understanding of work (Sandberg, 2000, p. 63).

5.3. Expertise and higher order work

Given that (diminishing marginal) improvements in performance continue indefinitely, some authorities have considered the conditions under which performance reaches a level that can be considered expert. In an investigation of expertise in diagnosing x-ray pictures Lesgold et al. (1988) demonstrated that experts display a greater capacity to invoke and refine schemas of interpretation, as well as deeper recognition-triggered reasoning, than novices, who do little more than attempt a literal perceptual interpretation. Proctor and Dutta (1995, p. 262) note that 'expertise typically is acquired through many years of intensive, deliberate practice in a particular domain, with 10 years typically given as the minimum time for expert levels of performance to be achieved'. While innate abilities are important in developing expertise, the special characteristics that define expertise are usually specific to that domain, suggesting that practice is more important (Ericsson, Krampe and Tesch-Romer, 1993; Ericsson and Smith, 1991). Nevertheless, certain characteristics appear to apply to experts in a range of domains: '(a) knowledge structures that enable … [them] to encode information in large meaningful chunks; (b) strategies that enable efficient coordination of the various components of task performance; and (c) metacognitive abilities that allow evaluation of progress' (Proctor and Dutta, 1995, p. 262).

Conceptual competences, including both cognitive and meta-competences, are often associated with higher level jobs involving more responsibility, but Gerber and Lankshear (2000, p. 4) argue that all 'workers become more effective when they reflect on their actions when doing their jobs. Such reflection is important in developing competence in one's work'. This notion is reinforced with an interpretative approach capable of incorporating tacit skills and knowledge. Billett (1993) analysed the nature of skilled work using the Australian (Mayer) key competencies and found many similarities across different classes of workers and, while the frequency varied across categories, the ability to use higher order forms of thinking was not restricted to professionals. Gerber (2000, p. 88-89) emphasises developing context-specific common sense through experiential learning and characterises highly effective workers as those who in addition to the practical common-sense knowledge 'also possess excellent theoretical knowledge', making them experts. The role of communication skills in sharing this expertise is obvious: 'Being good as an expert worker also has something to do with being a very good verbal and non-verbal communicator'. (Gerber, 2000, p. 91). However, the key feature that sets experts apart from others appears to be 'the existence and organisation of their knowledge rather than their ability to process that knowledge' (Billett, 2000, p. 135; but see also Anderson, 1982; Glaser, 1984; Wagner and Sternberg, 1986).

Elliott Jacques (1956; 1961; 1964) devised a measure of the level of work roles in terms of the 'time-span of discretion' (the longest targeted completion time for any of the tasks assigned), which he proposed as an alternative to job evaluation techniques in order better to capture different levels of responsibility. Individuals who have greater capability can undertake higher level work roles and so have a longer time-span of discretion. According to Jacques (1994, p. 7-8) 'individual working capability', comprises three aspects:

> Current potential capability ... the maximum level of work that that person could carry out at any given point in time ... [work that he or she valued doing and had been able to gain the necessary experience and skilled knowledge to perform]. ... this potential has at any time a maximum level determined by the person's maximum complexity of mental processing.
>
> Current applied capability ... the level of capability a person is actually applying at a given moment in some specific work. ... it is a function not only of that person's potential capability, but also of both the intensity of his or her commitment to doing that work, and the extent of his or her experience and skilled knowledge about it.
>
> Future potential capability ... the predicted level of potential capability that a person will possess at some specific time in the future. ... the potential capability grows throughout life from early childhood to old age along regular and predictable maturational pathways.

To assess the level at which an individual should be able to work, it is 'necessary to know not only the level of that person's potential capability but also how much he or she valued doing that work, and whether he or she had the necessary skilled knowledge for it' (Jacques, 1994, p. 21). In disaggregating applied capability, which is of most immediate relevance for discussing KSCs, Jacques (1994, p. 76-82) identifies three elements:

> Commitment to type of work ... in the sense of how much a person values doing the work; not in the generic sense of ethics and moral values. ... the more that individuals value the work they are doing, the more likely it will be they will maintain the attempt to apply their full potential. ...
>
> Skilled knowledge ... in relation to particular tasks affects our applied capability by influencing the effectiveness with which we can apply the potential capability that we are committing to the work. The greater the relevant knowledge, the greater our effectiveness will be. Skilled knowledge has to do with the tools with which to do the work. ... By skill we refer to our ability to use the knowledge and the procedures of which we have knowledge automatically. ...

> Temperamental characteristics … – personality or enduring temperamental characteristics; such qualities as initiative, aggressiveness, flexibility, emotional warmth, optimism, curiosity, reliability, caring. … The indirect effect occurs via the impact of these enduring personal characteristics upon the development of our values, the values that determine what we choose to do and that affect our intensity of commitment in different circumstances.

Notwithstanding the unusual terminology, a function of the period in which most of the work was done (in Glacier Metal during the 1960s) much of this approach is echoed in modern concepts of KSCs. Applied capability is akin to an umbrella use of competence (KSC in our terminology) since it is concerned with actual performance in the workplace. 'Commitment' (which generally nowadays is used in the context of loyalty to a particular organisation) in the sense used by Jacques may be better termed motivation, which clearly affects performance but which we distinguish from KSCs. 'Skilled knowledge' entails both knowledge (cognitive competence) and skills (functional competence), which we distinguish analytically. 'Temperamental characteristics' clearly relate to the psycho-social domain of behaviours and attitudes, which we characterise as social competence.

5.4. Assessment of levels of KSCs

Most attempts to assess levels of KSCs assume the underlying characteristics (whether knowledge, skills or behavioural attributes) are associated with job performance (Herman and Kenyon, 1987; Nitardy and McLean, 2002), whether this is just adequate achievement of work objectives (Green, 1999) or high performance (Mirabile, 1997). Since competence (in the broader sense of KSA manifest in the work context) is specific to an occupation, it is 'by definition, related to the technical aspects of performance' (Stewart and Hamlin, 1994, p. 4) and 'assessment of competence should be grounded in performance in the workplace' (Norris, 1991, p. 4). This is the philosophy of the UK NVQ/SVQ system, although the extent to which assessment is actually grounded in the workplace has been questioned (Canning, 2000; Field, 1995; Purcell, 2001).

Boon and van der Klink (2002, p. 4) define competence even more broadly, including 'innate abilities, emotions, attitudes, skills and knowledge, and the motivation and ability to apply in certain context'. Gangani, McLean and Braden (2004, p. 1111) similarly include 'the skills, knowledge, behaviours, personal characteristics and motivations associated with success in a job'. This adds to the conceptual confusion, since motivation is clearly not a part of competence. A person is said to be competent if they have the requisite KSCs, but whether or not they are motivated is a function of a whole range of external and internal factors. Performance can be viewed as a function of KSCs, interacting with motivation (the individual's predisposition to perform) and organisation (the work conditions facilitating or hampering, performance).

As Weinert (1999) notes, while motivational incentives in the environment are important in learning and developing competence, motivation should not be considered a part of competence:

> The developmental status and potential for actualising a specific cognitive competence is thus always also a function of motivational readiness for systematic learning. Extending the competence concept to include a motivational dimension complicates the defining, measuring and operationalising the competence construct, even as it adds to its theoretical and pedagogical attractiveness of such an approach (Weinert, 1999, p. 20).

In considering the assessment of KSCs, there is also the question of progression and development and this can be extrapolated to reference levels. In everyday language, if an individual is competent, they can adequately perform the task or job in question, but they are not necessarily demonstrating any particular expertise in executing that role. As Tate (1995b, p. 82) notes, 'the word "competent" suffers from the connotation of bare sufficiency or adequacy, as opposed to expertise'. In this respect, the UK notion of threshold competence may be contrasted with the US approach where competence is against the yardstick of the best performers. The term incompetent, is usually applied to a person who is inept at the tasks they perform, and likely to remain so, whereas 'not yet competent', the terminology of the UK VQ framework, implies the individual is expected to attain competence as a result of further development and training. Burgoyne (1988a) questioned this dichotomy and it is perhaps more realistic to consider a continuum of degrees of competence, with a threshold of competence where the individual meets the defined standards, but has scope for developing further skills, knowledge and understanding. Several authors have incorporated a developmental dimension in their definitions of competence, recognising the need for continual renewal and adaptation in developing competence (Eraut, 1994; Nitardy and McLean, 2002; Norris, 1991; Wood and Powers, 1987). This developmental dimension is reflected in the range indicators associated with competence at different VQ levels and with the use of competence frameworks for forecasting future skills needs (Daniels, Erickson and Dalik, 2001; Winterton and Winterton, 2002b; Winterton et al., 2000). Such an approach is also consistent with an organisation's continuous improvement strategies and the notion of individual progression through lifelong learning.

6. European experience with KSCs

Given the different traditions of VET systems and economic conditions between EU Member States, it is understandable that there is currently no common approach to defining learning outcomes in terms of KSCs. The following review considers some of the approaches and recent developments that are relevant to establishing a common typology of KSCs. The United Kingdom is considered initially because it was the first to develop a VET framework based primarily on competence-based outcomes.

6.1. The UK: a predominantly functional approach

Recognising endemic deficiencies of skill formation in the United Kingdom, governments during the 1980s introduced a competence-based approach to VET to establish a nation-wide unified system of work-based qualifications (Heidemann et al., 1998; Winterton and Winterton, 1998). This VET reform was driven by the adoption of a competence-based qualifications framework and definitions of respective qualifications; this subsequently influenced similar developments in other English-speaking countries [3] and in the European Union [4].

The vocational qualifications (VQs) [5] created under the new framework were based on occupational standards of competence, grounded in functional analysis of occupations in various contexts (Debling, 1991; Jessup, 1991; Mansfield and Mitchell, 1996). The Management Standards, for example, were developed and tested with over 3 000 managers, across a range of sectors (Frank, 1991) making the Management Charter Initiative (MCI) competence framework the 'best researched of its kind' (Fowler, 1994). However, as Jubb and Rowbotham (1997) note:

---

[3] Notably Australia, Canada, Cyprus, Malta and New Zealand.
[4] Finland, for example.
[5] In England and Wales, these are known as National vocational qualifications (NVQs) and in Scotland as Scottish vocational qualifications (SVQs). While the term vocational qualifications (VQs) normally covers all such qualifications, whether or not they are competence based, in this section of the paper we are referring particularly to the competence-based qualifications (NVQs and SVQs) in the new VET framework.

A single list of competences represents only a theoretical blueprint, albeit derived from observations of actual management behaviour. That template for effective performance also represents performance at a point in time, i.e. a list may include behaviours that appeared effective during observation, but in terms of achieving long-term goals were perhaps ineffective.

Standards are defined as statements of competence written to describe desired performance outcomes. The emphasis is on functional competence and the ability to demonstrate performance to the standards required of employment in a work context (Knasel and Meed, 1994). The definition of occupational competence provided by the Manpower Services Commission (MSC, 1986) and adopted by Investors in People (1995, p. 41) was 'the ability to perform activities in the jobs within an occupation, to the standards expected in employment'. However, the definition also included 'mastery of skills and understanding' and 'aspects of personal effectiveness'. As Mansfield and Mitchell (1996, p. 46) note, this definition 'appears to include a mix of models: work expectations, input measures (knowledge and skills) and psychological attributes'. Also, Mansfield (2004, p. 303) believes that from the outset there were two parallel views of competence: a narrow view in which 'competent people were those who followed rules and procedures without question – competence meant compliance'; and a broader view that emphasised flexibility, adaptability and the need for individuals to take more responsibility.

Indeed the original management standards were supplemented by an MCI 'competency model defining behavioural performance indicators. Nevertheless, the MSC definition of competence was subsequently adopted as the official employment department approach in defining occupational standards as 'a description of something which a person who works in a given occupational area should be able to do ... [and] able to demonstrate' (Training agency, 1988, p. 5; Employment department and NCVQ, 1991). A government review of vocational qualifications in 1996 (Beaumont, 1996) expanded the definition of competence as 'the ability to apply knowledge, understanding and skills in performing to the standards required in employment. This includes solving problems and meeting changing demand'. Beaumont also recommended simplifying the terminology and structure, reducing bureaucracy, sharing good practice, providing more guidance on assessment and a review of outcome-related funding, which had distorted delivery. The National Council for vocational qualifications (NCVQ, now Qualifications and curriculum authority, QCA) continued to improve the NVQ system but non-NVQ/SVQ vocational qualifications remained popular (Robinson, 1996) and take-up of the new qualifications less than anticipated in government education and training targets.

National occupational standards describe good practice, what is required in the workplace rather than what people are like, and play a role in linking organisational strategy and individual learning needs; hence they are used to design education and training curricula and qualifications. They can also be used more widely in managing and developing organisations and individuals, for job design, recruitment, individual and team development, career planning and appraisal. Occupational standards identify key roles, which are then broken down into several units of competence. These are further subdivided into elements of competence and for each element of competence, performance criteria are defined which form the basis of assessment, with range indicators provided for guidance. Occupational standards are firmly rooted in the reality of work (Mansfield, 1993) and employers play a leading part in their validation. Also, in unionised sectors there was trade union involvement in establishing and maintaining occupational standards, even under the Conservatives (Winterton and Winterton, 1994). Nevertheless, participation by employers in the formal vocational qualifications system has been far from universal (Matlay, 2000), partly because of a perceived lack of relevance to specific employer needs (Konrad, 2000) and partly due to the bureaucracy associated with assessment procedures. Assessment for VQs involves accrediting the competence of individuals against actual performance in the workplace, which was designed to ensure continued relevance to the work situation (Miller, 1991). Self-evaluation against competence statements has been shown to be reliable provided these are modelled on the job (Hansson, 2001), yet there is evidence (Bell and Dale, 1999) that VQ assessment fails to capture many of the outcomes of informal learning, because workplace assessors are not adequately prepared.

Another criticism of VQs related to their apparent lack of adequate theoretical underpinning as the competence-based approach was concerned only with demonstrating competence (functional skills) in the workplace and not the systematic acquisition of knowledge. Underlying knowledge has always played a major part in craft qualifications awarded by such bodies as the City and Guilds of London Institute and this continued to be the case under the new VQs, as city and guilds became one of the awarding institutions. The criticism probably also reflects the resistance of educational institutions to a competence-based approach. Much of the early UK literature on NVQs was dominated by academic critiques which were hostile to the competence-based approach per se (Bates, 1995; Ecclestone, 1999; 2000; Jones and Moore, 1995; Wolf, 1995; 1998). Hyland (1994) described NVQs as fundamentally flawed and inappropriate to current and future education and training needs. Smithers (1993) attacked the underpinning knowledge of NVQs compared with VQs in countries like Germany and did not disguise his opposition to a learner-centred approach. Some 25 years ago, the American management association (AMA) identified five clusters of competences which were believed to be associated with effective managerial behaviour (Hayes, 1979; 1980a; 1980b) and these prompted the American association of colleges and schools of business to promote the competency approach in US business schools (Albanese, 1989). By contrast, the competence-based management standards developed by the management charter initiative had less influence on UK business schools (IoM, 1994).

While the main approach in the United Kingdom remains one of functional competence, some employers developed their own competence frameworks for managers or adopted other generic models instead of using the MCI standards (Carrington, 1994; Hirsh and Strebler, 1994; Iles, 1993; Stringfellow, 1994). Some organisations adopted the Hay McBer competency framework in preference to the competences embodied in the management standards (Mathewman, 1995; Cockerill, 1989). Diverse competence models have been introduced in relation to competence-based pay systems (Reilly, 2003) and especially for competence-based management development (Strebler and Bevan, 1996). According to Mansfield (2004, p. 303), this demonstrates that a dichotomy arose in the use of competence: 'one for narrow and routine jobs and the other for broader and more responsible jobs. The 'competency' (personal characteristics) approach quickly filled the gap by claiming ownership of managerial and professional occupations'. Significantly, several leading critics of the narrowness of the NVQ approach did not support the personal characteristics approach as an alternative but argued for the need to complement functional competence with basic knowledge and other elements derived from the reality of work (Stewart and Hamblin, 1992a; 1992b; 1993).

Hodkinson and Issitt (1995, p. 149) argued for a more holistic approach to competence in the caring professions, integrating knowledge, understanding, values and skills that 'reside within the person who is the practitioner'. Similarly, Cheetham and Chivers (1996; 1998) developed a holistic model of professional competence, comprising five sets of inter-connected competences and competencies. Their holistic competence framework comprises five dimensions:

(a) cognitive competence, including theory and concepts, as well as informal tacit knowledge gained experientially. Knowledge (know-that) underpinned by understanding (know-why), is distinguished from competence;

(b) functional competences (skills or know-how), those things that a person who works in a given occupational area should be able to do ... [and] able to demonstrate;

(c) personal competency (behavioural competencies, know how to behave), defined as a 'relatively enduring characteristic of a person causally related to effective or superior performance in a job' (Spencer 1995, p. 144);

(d) ethical competencies, defined as 'the possession of appropriate personal and professional values and the ability to make sound judgements based upon these in work-related situations' (Cheetham and Chivers 1996, p. 24);

(e) meta-competencies, concerned with the ability to cope with uncertainty, as well as with learning and reflection (Brown, 1993; Nordhaug, 1993).

This framework was applied in an analysis of the future skills needs of managers in the United Kingdom undertaken for the Department of Education and Skills (Winterton et al., 2000), and, using a modified version (6), in a further study undertaken for the Inland Revenue (Winterton and Winterton, 2002a). This later research into implementing management standards in 16 organisations found that 9 were using the functional competences based on the management standards only, 2 were using behavioural competency frameworks and 5 had combined functional competence and behavioural competency to introduce hybrid competence models. This evidence suggests that in the United Kingdom too, the concept of competence is being broadened to capture underlying knowledge and behaviours rather than simply functional competences associated with specific occupations.

6.2. France: a multidimensional approach

The competence movement started later in France, during the 1980s, and became particularly influential from the 1990s. The emergence and development of competence has passed through several stages: after the first appearance of the idea within organisations, came the development of instruments and tools for HRM practitioners and consultants, then the conceptualisation of competence as a theoretical concern and finally more critical approaches. The major development of competence-based practice appeared in 1984, linked to the need to develop new competences and the role of enterprises in developing them (Cannac and CEGOS, 1985). Gilbert (2003) traces the history of the management of competence à la française, which carries the imprint of national culture (in a context of a right to vocational training and the important role of collective agreements), so the strong global influence of the McClelland approach is much less evident in France.

At the end of the 1980s, faced with the continued challenge of restructuring of enterprises, the ANPE (*Agence nationale pour l'emploi*) launched ROME (*Répertoire Opérationnel des Métiers et des Emplois*) which was modified in 1993 and gave a central role to competence. Several key texts appeared around this time (Le Boterf, 1994; Levy-Leboyer, 1996; Merle, 1996; Minet, Parlier and de Witte, 1994) when a more structured approach to competence was also developed in several enterprises, notably by Sollac in Dunkerque,

---

(6) Ethical competencies were subsumed under personal competency, as in the MCI personal competency model.

Propharm and Crédit Mutuel de Bretagne, and later at Renault (Haddadj and Besson, 2000b). At the same time, HRM was evolving towards *Gestion Prévisionnelle des Emplois et des Compétences* (GPEC) accompanying organisational transformation in which human resources became considered as invisible assets producing competitive advantage (Raoult, 1991). With this approach, it is argued that HRM began using individual evaluation to replace the logic of qualification with competence (Durand, J.P., 2000; Pochet, 1999) with a consequent increase in flexibility that is sometimes seen as a risk to job security (Arnaud and Lauriol, 2002). From the management of competence through GPEC evolved *Emplois types en dynamique* (ETED) as a method that explicitly recognises the rapidity of changes in competence requirements (Mandon, 1990; 1998; Mandon and Liaroutzos, 1994).

Further impetus was given to the competence movement during the 1990s when the state introduced a right for individuals to have a *bilan de compétences* undertaken by educational organisations to provide a basis for personal development in their occupation (Joras, 2002; Vind et al., 2004). The concept of competence featured increasingly in HRM since the mid 1990s, both in research and practice and has been associated with several different normative models and various practices (Minet, 1994; Parlier, 1994). Competence also became more focused on HRD (Dousset, 1990) and the instruments for developing and measuring competences began to appear (Deitrich, 2003; Klarsfeld and Roques, 2003; Paraponaris, 2003; Trépo and Ferrary, 1997; 1998). Competence-based pay was introduced in some heavy industries (Brochier and Oiry, 2003; Klarsfeld and Saint-Onge, 2000).

The competence movement has gained further ground following the initiatives of the employers' association MEDEF (*Mouvement des Entreprises de France*). The MEDEF initiative, *Objectif competences*, started five years ago, was formally launched in 2002 with the support of the European Commission and provided extensive practical information on the use of competence within enterprises. This was accompanied by more academic publications (Brochier, 2002; Dupray, Guitton and Monchatre, 2003; Gangloff, 2000; Klarsfeld and Oiry, 2003; Lepron, 2001; Quélin and Arrègle, 2000; Zarifian, 2000), and a more critical-analytical approach from several observers (Arnaud and Lauriol, 2002; Estellat, 2003; Louart, 2003; Martin, 2003; Parlier, Perrien and Thierry, 2000).

Haddadj and Besson (2000a) note that from an epistemological perspective, the logic of competence is polarized into two distinct directions: an individual approach, centred on individual behaviours, and a collective approach, centred on building the required competence in an organisation. Most definitions of competence fall between two extremes: competence as a universal attribute, such as literacy, and competence in terms of individual capacity, which is only found in the work context (Klarsfeld, 2000). Zarifian (1999a) designed a model for developing and applying competence within the so-called *organisation qualifiante*, in which training and development is linked with the analysis of knowledge and skills that form an essential, and inseparable, part of work tasks. There are several reasons for adopting management by competence, but the central objective remains the improvement of performance and productivity (Bataille, 2001; Zarifian, 1999b) and this presupposes several conditions to create the organisational context in which competence delivers the benefits (Amadieu and Cadin, 1996; Zarifian, 1999a).

Several French authors have compared the French approach with the 'Anglo-Saxon' (often only American in practice) approach. Defelix, Martin and Retour (2001) believe the Anglo-Saxon approach to be analytically more precise and complex, particularly in relation to soft competencies (behaviours). Tremblay and Sire (1999, p. 131) characterise the Anglo-Saxon approach as dealing with hard competences (knowledge and skills) or *compétences essentielles* as well as soft competences (behaviours, traits and motive) or *compétences différentielles*. The French approach is generally more comprehensive, considering *savoir* (*compétences théoriques*, i.e. knowledge), *savoir-faire* (*compétences pratiques*, i.e. functional competences) and *savoir-être* (*compétences sociales et comportementales*, i.e. behavioural competencies, see Bellier, 2004). Tremblay and Sire (1999) note a strong concordance between the United Kingdom use of functional competence and the French *savoir-faire* and between the US use of soft competences, as in the Hay approach, and the French *savoir-être*.

Dejoux (1999) comments that in France while the notion of individual competence has not yet generated a general, empirically-validated theory, there is none the less a consensus definition based on the minimal three dimensions already mentioned. These three dimensions rest on the concepts of knowledge (*savoir* and *connaissance*), a component based on experience (*savoir faire* or *savoir agir*) and a behavioural component (*savoir être* or *la faculté de s'adapter*). According to Cazal and Deitrich (2003) this *triptyque* is largely confined to HRD, although it has occasionally appeared in the vocabulary of those concerned with strategy (Durand, T., 2000).

6.3. Germany: emphasising the unity of the craft

The German dual system of VET has long been viewed as a model for Europe and has had a determining influence on Austria, Hungary and Slovenia and, to a lesser extent, the Scandinavian countries. While competence (*Kompetenz*) was implicit in the system, the main emphasis was on specifying the necessary learning inputs, rather than outcomes, to master a trade. Occupational competence is rooted in the concept of *Beruf* (usually translated as occupation, but encompassing the traditions of the craft from the trade and craft guilds), which defines vocational training theory and associated pedagogy (Meyer, 2002). Within this tradition, modularisation and generic competences are regarded with suspicion since these may damage the unity of the craft (Ertl, 2002).

During the 1960s, 'qualification' (*Qualifikation*) was understood not as the possession of a certificate but as the mastery of specific life-situations or occupational tasks. The concept of 'key qualifications' (*Schlüsselqualifikationen*) appeared from the 1980s, and still dominates today. Here the emphasis is no longer on concrete specialised situational demands, but on the person's characteristics, experience and knowledge. The key qualifications expected of a skilled production worker, for example, include analytical skills for interpreting information and sophisticated social-communicative competences. As decision-making competences are increasingly transferred to lower levels in the occupational hierarchy, social skills increasingly belong to the key qualifications, alongside work-process related skills. Personal competences, such as ability to act autonomously and to solve problems independently, flexibility, ability to cooperate, practical ethics and moral maturity also belong to *Schlüsselqualifikationen*.

While *Qualifikation* signifies the ability to master concrete (generally professional) situation requirements (so is clearly application-oriented), *Kompetenz* refers to the capacity of a person to act and is subject-oriented (Anold et al., 2001, p. 176). *Kompetenz* is also more holistic, comprising not only content or subject knowledge and ability, but also extra-subject or transversal abilities (often still described as *Schlüsselqualifikationen* but increasingly also as *Methodkompetenz, Sozialkompetenz, Personalkompetenz*). During the 1980s the term *Kompetenz* was further differentiated so that more or less all facets of training were stylised to independent competences, such as 'media-competence' (*Medienkompetenz*), 'ecological-competence' (*ökologischer Kompetenz*) and 'democracy-competence' (*Demokratiekompetenz*).

In 1996 the German education system adopted an 'action competence' (*Handlungskompetenz*) approach, moving from subject (inputs) to competence (outcomes) and curricula specifying learning fields (*Lernfelder*) rather than occupation related knowledge and skills content (Straka 2002; 2004). According to the Federal Ministry of Education and Research, *Kompetenz* is concerned with capacity to act (*Handlungsvermögen*) and in the occupational sense this is expressed as vocational action competence (*beruflicher Handlungskompeten*). The (sector specific) Social Partner Organisations do propose the rules for state recognised apprenticeships and training profiles and these are officially regulated jointly by the Federal government and the *Länder* governments represented by the *Kultus Minister Konferenz* (KMK) (some 350 training profiles currently exist). The standard typology of competences decided upon by the KMK in 2000 appears at the beginning of every new vocational training curriculum, elaborating vocational action competence (*Handlungskompetenz*) in terms of domain or subject-competence (*Fachkompetenz*), personal competence (*Personalkompetenz*) and social competence (*Sozialkompetenz*).

Domain competence describes the willingness and ability, on the basis of subject-specific knowledge and skills, to carry out tasks and solve problems and to judge the results in a way that is goal-oriented, appropriate, methodological and independent. General cognitive competence (*Sachkompetenz*), the ability to think and act in an insightful and problem-solving way, is a prerequisite for developing *Fachkompetenz*, which therefore includes both cognitive and functional competences.

Personal competence describes the willingness and ability, as an individual personality, to understand, analyse and judge the development chances, requirements and limitations in the family, job and public life, to develop one's own skills and to decide on and develop life plans. It includes personal characteristics like independence, critical abilities, self-confidence, reliability, responsibility and awareness of duty, and professional and ethical values. *Personalkompetenz* therefore includes both cognitive and social competences. In some accounts, self-competence (*Selbstkompetenz*) is distinguished, as the ability to act in a morally self-determined humane way, including the assertion of a positive self-image and developing moral judgement.

Social competence describes the willingness and ability to experience and shape relationships, to identify and understand benefits and tensions, and to interact with others in a rational and conscientious way, including developing social responsibility and solidarity. *Sozialkompetenz* therefore includes both functional and social competences. A balance of subject, personal and social competence is the prerequisite for 'method and learning competence' (*Methodenkompetenz* and *Lernkompetenz*). Method competence may be viewed as an extension of *Sachkompetenz* and *Fachkompetenz* arising from the implementation of transversal strategies and processes of invention and problem-solving. This approach clearly influenced developing the idea of 'work process knowledge' (Boreham, 2002). Learning competence equates to the meta-competence 'learning how to learn'.

There are currently 350 occupational profiles in Germany defined to a common format elaborating the competences required in terms of the above. Occupational profiles are divided into fields of activity defining the requisite skills and knowledge of an occupation; these are made concrete in the training plan (devised by the training company) and the skeleton (national) school curriculum, which is elaborated in further detail in the *Länder*, since responsibility for vocational education is regionally devolved. In June 2002 the Federal Ministry of education and research agreed to establish national educational standards in core subjects as part of a series of school reforms associated with the move to more output focused education. In 2004, a report by a wide range of experts considered the expectations of schools in terms of educational goals and learning outcomes, arguing that 'educational goals are relatively general statements about the knowledge, abilities and skills, as well as attitudes, values, interests and motivations, that schools are expected to impart' (Klieme et al., 2004, p. 15). According to these experts, 'competency models serve, on the one hand, to describe the learning outcomes expected of students of given ages in specific subjects. Conversely, they map out possible "routes to knowledge and skills" based on sound scientific insights' (Klieme et al., 2004, p. 64). Arguing that competency models thus provide a framework for operationalising educational goals, they conclude that these models bridge the gap between abstract educational goals and concrete occupational tasks.

6.4. Experiences of other European countries

In recent years many Member States have moved towards learning outcomes and competence-based VET systems and qualifications, sometimes following closely one of the above models and occasionally developing distinctive approaches. Competence-based occupational profiles and/or qualification frameworks already exist or are under development in most of the 15 'old' EU Member States and are being promoted in those of the 10 'new' EU Member States that had not already adopted such an approach.

Austria, with VET traditions like those of Germany, retained the concept of key qualifications (*Schlüsselqualifikationen*) defining these as transversal functional and professional qualifications, including non-subject specific abilities and aspects of personality formation, which have significance beyond the specific occupation (Archan and Tutschek, 2002). The latest training regulations governing teaching of key qualifications to apprentices note that the personality formation of apprentices must be addressed when training subject knowledge and skills to ensure they have the necessary social competence (such as openness, ability to work in a team and handle conflicts), personal competence (such as self-evaluation, self-confidence, independence, ability to work under pressure), method competence (such as presentation skills, rhetorical skills in the German language, ability to make oneself understood in basic English) and competence for self-organised learning (such as willingness, knowledge of methods, ability to select appropriate media and materials). These are normally grouped under three headings: cognitive, social and personal competences. Cognitive competence (*Sachkompetenz*) is defined as knowledge, skills and abilities that may be used in the specific occupation as well as transversally, and skills and abilities for mastering tasks and developing appropriate problem solving strategies. Thus theoretical thinking, method competence (including learning techniques) and general vocationally-oriented skills such as IT, workplace safety and business management are subsumed under *Sachkompetenz*. Social competence (*Sozialkompetenz*) is largely concerned with dealing with others and is defined as the ability and willingness to cooperate, to interact with others responsibly and to behave in a group and relationally oriented way. Personal competence (*Selbstkompetenz*) comprises key qualifications for dealing with oneself and is defined in terms of ability and willingness to develop personally, and to develop skills, motivation and attitudes to work and the wider world.

In the Netherlands, the Advisory Committee for Education and Labour Market published a proposal in 1999 entitled 'shift to core competences' in response to the employers' argument that the skills needed for work are best obtained through work rather than formal education. As a result, detailed competence profiles (*beroepscompetentieprofiel*) have been defined for 291 occupations, specifying in each case a broad job description (*beroepsbeschrijving*), and vocational competences with associated success criteria divided into core functional or technical tasks (*kerntaken*) and core behavioural tasks (*kernopgaven*). These are further subdivided into specific competences associated with the job (*beroepscompetentie*), some of which are a hybrid of functional and behavioural aspects. Each *beroepscompetentie* is classed as having one or more of the following 'dimensions' (*dimensies)*:

- the profession-specific method (or process) dimension (*vakmatig-methodische dimensie*) refers to professional competences such as techniques with which to carry out core functions and core tasks in an appropriate manner;
- the administrative-organisational and strategic dimension (*BOS, bestuurlijk-organisatorische en strategische dimensie*) refers to professional competences directed at professional functioning in the context of work organisations;
- the social-communicative dimension (*social-communicatieve dimensie*) refers to professional competences directed at establishing and maintaining contacts, cooperation, team work, etc.;
- the development dimension (*ontwikkelingsdimensie*) refers to professional competences that contribute to the development of an individual, team, occupation, organisation or business.

Knowledge or cognitive competence is assumed to underpin both the functional and behavioural and is not separately identified in the common format, as described in COLO (2003).

Finland adopted a competence-based approach in upper secondary vocational education in 1994 and since 1999 competence-based qualifications have been regulated by the Act (*Laki ammatillisesta aikuiskoulutuksesta* 631/1998) and Decree (*Asetus ammatillisesta aikuiskoulutuksesta* 812/1998) on vocational adult education. The Ministry of Education decides which qualifications are to be included in the qualifications structure, which currently includes 357 qualifications (175 of them further vocational qualifications and 129 specialist vocational qualifications). The typology of vocational competence distinguishes core competences common to all fields (such as learning, communication and ethical skills), and vocational competences relating to seven broad sectors of economic activity. For each sector, the vocational competences are grouped into knowledge that forms the foundation of work, occupational safety and work processes, with the associated working methods, tools and materials.

In Portugal, the secondary education system has been revised by the Ministry of Education and the curricula are being designed to achieve learning outcomes specified in terms of cognitive competences (*competências cognitivas*), functional competences (*competências funcionais*) and social competences (*competências sociais*). The vocational training research and development body, the Institute for quality in training.

(IQT, formerly INOFOR), is diagnosing skill trends and training needs and developing occupational profiles for all economic sectors. These occupational profiles are competence-based, using a typology like that in secondary education, which IQT staff regard as close to the French approach: knowledge (*savoir/compétences théorique*), technical know-how (*savoir faire*) and social and relational skills (*savoir-être/compétence sociale et comportamentale*). There is not yet a National framework of qualifications, but from this work on occupational profiles IQT are now developing a methodology for the production of a National catalogue of qualifications which will include competence standards for each qualification.

Similarly, in Spain a basic law on qualifications is being developed and the National catalogue of occupational qualifications outlines 84 occupational profiles (*cualificaciones profesionales*) grouped into occupational families and assigned to levels 1 to 5. According to Article 4 of the Royal Decree 1128/2003, which regulates the National catalogue, 'the levels of occupational qualification are established according to the professional competence required by the productive activities in accordance with criteria of knowledge, initiative, autonomy, responsibility and complexity, among others, of the activity'. Occupational profiles begin with 'general competence' (*competencia general*), a brief description of the essential functions of the occupation, then 'units of competence' (*unidades de competencia*) are outlined in terms of elements of competence establishing the behaviour expected of the person and the desired outcomes. Performance criteria (*realizaciones profesionales y criterios de realización*) are also defined in terms of what is needed to meet the standards of employment, to guide evaluation of occupational competence. The professional context (*entorno professional*) is also outlined, describing the media of production, products and results of the work, information utilised or generated and other such elements considered necessary for carrying out occupational activities. Finally 'associated training' (*formación asociada*) is described in the form of modules corresponding to each of the numbered units of competence. Units of competence only describe functions and desired outcomes and there is no mention of basic knowledge or social competences. In Spanish, *cualification* is normally used in the sense of occupational profile, although as elsewhere it can also refer to the certificate recognising a person's ability. Similarly, *competencia* may refer to competence in a general sense or to specific skills, but these relate almost exclusively to functional tasks. The Organic Act 5/2002 on qualifications and vocational training (BOE No. 147 of 20 June 2002) in Title 1, Article 7, defines occupational qualification as 'the set of occupational competences with meaning for the occupation that can be acquired through training in modules or other types of training and through on-the-job experience,' and occupational competence as 'the set of knowledge and abilities (*conocimientos y capacidades*) that enable one to exercise the occupation pursuant to the demands of employment'.

In Norway (which is outside the EU but a member of EFTA) the Ministry of Education ran a project entitled *Realkompetanse* between 1999 and 2002 to enable adults to document non-formal and informal learning via a portfolio of evidence and a workplace competence card documenting what the employee is able to do as part of their job. The main areas of work responsibility are described with a specification of the professional skills (occupational competences) needed, personal capabilities, social and personal skills (social competences) and management skills (Straka, 2004).

7. A prototype typology of knowledge, skills and competence

This review has demonstrated the growing interest in multi-dimensional frameworks of KSCs. Functional and cognitive competences are increasingly being augmented by social or behavioural competences and there appears to be a general movement towards the more holistic approaches that have been associated with Germany and France, where knowledge, skills and social attitudes and behaviours are viewed as related dimensions of competence.

7.1. A unified typology of KSCs

Developing a typology for ECVET should draw on perceived good practice within the EU. The challenge is to develop a consistent and coherent typology of KSCs in a context where even within countries there is apparent diversity in the approaches to competence. The holistic approach to competence (Gonczi, 1994; Tovey, 1993), combining knowledge, skills and attitudes, is gaining ground over narrower approaches and several authorities are developing more integrated approaches along these lines (Engle et al., 2001; Hager, 1994). Where interpretive approaches have also been influential, competence is viewed as being multifaceted, holistic and integrated (Gerbe and Velde, 1996; Velde, 1997; 1999). Such an approach offers a unifying framework for defining the KSCs that are necessary for particular occupations and so provides a starting point for establishing a typology of KSCs for the ECVET. The four dimensions of competence are distinguished in Figure 3 which forms an overarching framework to begin developing a typology of KSCs.

The first three dimensions, cognitive, functional and social competences, are fairly universal and are clearly consistent with the French approach (*savoir*, *savoir faire*, *savoir être*) as well as the longstanding KSA (knowledge, skills and attitudes) of the training profession derived from Bloom's taxonomy of learning. In developing new methods of training evaluation, for example, Kraiger, Ford and Salas (1993) similarly draw on cognitive, skill-based and affective theories of learning outcomes. Thus, knowledge and understanding are captured by cognitive competence; skills are captured by functional competence, while attitudes and behaviours are captured by social competence. Meta-competence

Figure 3:   **Unified typology of KSCs**

	occupational	personal
conceptual	cognitive competence (knowledge)	meta-competence (facilitating learning)
operational	functional competence (skills)	social competence (attitudes and behaviours)

is different from the first three dimensions since it is concerned with facilitating the acquisition of the other substantive competences. Further, while the distinction between these dimensions can be made analytically, in practice, not only must a person have underlying knowledge, functional skills and appropriate social behaviour to be effective at work, the competences required of an occupation are also invariably described in multi-dimensional terms.

Given the TWG decision to retain 'knowledge, skills and competences' (KSCs) as a unified statement, we have incorporated meta-competencies within the social competences category. The problem with using the term KSCs is that without further qualification, the term competence alone is too broad: in the United Kingdom and Ireland competence is generally understood as the ability to demonstrate in a work context, the necessary skills (functional competences), usually with appropriate basic knowledge (cognitive competences) and sometimes appropriate social competences (behavioural and attitudinal competences). For conceptual clarity the four dimensions distinguished above are important, but by this expedient of incorporating meta-competencies with social ones we arrive at a horizontal dimension that is consistent with the work of the TWG to date. However, using the term competence as a short-hand for social competence is potentially problematic because the term is most commonly used as a general term for demonstrating requisite knowledge and skills as well as appropriate behaviour *in a work context*. We therefore strongly recommend that in the interests of analytical precision, ECVET adopts the terminology of cognitive competence, functional competence and social competence.

7.2. Operationalising the typology

The above outline of the broad typology of KSCs represents a starting point for developing a prototype typology of learning outcomes for ECVET. Using such a framework of learning outcomes, educational and work-based provision can be more closely aligned, exploiting the synergy between formal education and experiential learning to develop professional competence. However, for the typology to be of practical use there is a major task of assessing the extent to which existing typologies of learning outcomes and qualifications frameworks can be accommodated within such an overall typology, when considered at a more detailed level.

To make the typology operational, national and sector frameworks must therefore be examined in more detail to test the practical potential of the typology of KSCs in specific sectors and occupations. The overall architecture of the prototype typology of KSCs has been agreed by the TWG with a matrix approach to accommodate different levels and the range of KSCs that need to be developed or demonstrated at each level. There have been extensive discussions of the optimum number of reference levels capable of accommodating on a best-fit basis the levels defined in existing competence and qualifications frameworks. Many levels would make a precise fit with existing frameworks easy, but risk an over-complex system, while a few levels would be more straightforward but more difficult to apply to existing frameworks. In the event, an eight-level framework was proposed in the QCA study and endorsed by the TWG, which agreed that the eight levels were broadly compatible with the ISCED and Cedefop levels and even with ISCO and the new levels framework proposed for the recognition of qualifications and regulated professions [7]. Subsequent discussion has considered the value of sub-levels to increase flexibility and accommodate such differences as between Danish and UK apprenticeships, both seen as level 4 programmes although the Danish apprenticeship is significantly broader and deeper in content and coverage than the United Kingdom one.

The levels increase in complexity from level 1, covering learning normally acquired during compulsory education, to level 8, covering qualifications that recognise a leading expert in a highly specialised field dealing with complex situations [8]. The general level descriptors are shown in Annex 2. An outline of the matrix is shown in Table 1.

Within this overall architecture selected frameworks can be used to populate the matrix with a series of specific descriptors for the occupation or sector. Not all levels will be appropriate in a given sector or occupational group; equally some KSCs' horizontal dimensions may not feature at all in some cases (although most would be expected to have some requirements in all three dimensions). At this stage it is not proposed to include sub-levels or introduce the complication of different degrees of competence, except where range indicators already exist, although the framework should be capable of this further refinement as it develops.

---

[7] See the respective directive proposal of the Commission from spring 2002.
[8] See DG Education and Culture note 'Developing common reference levels to underpin a European qualifications framework', 24.9.2004.

Table 1: **Matrix of typology of KSCs**

Level	Cognitive competence (knowledge)	Functional competence (skills)	Social and meta-competence (behaviours and attitudes)
Level 8			
Level 7			
Level 6			
Level 5			
Level 4			
Level 3			
Level 2			
Level 1			

To test the utility of the prototype typology it is necessary to explore the scope for integrating existing classifications at international, national and sector levels. The amount of detail in descriptors of what someone should know, what they should be able to do and how they should behave, to be considered competent at a particular level in a particular occupation, must also be agreed. If the typology is under-specified it risks insufficient precision to be operable; if it is overspecified it risks becoming unusable and more difficult to establish zones of mutual trust within each part of the matrix.

7.3. National frameworks of KSCs

The national qualifications frameworks introduced in Ireland and Scotland are particularly important as they have established levels that integrate VET and HE, thus under the Bologna-Copenhagen process joined up lifelong learning is possible. The Scottish framework has 12 levels and the Irish framework has 10, in contrast with the 8 levels agreed as European reference levels. The question of fitting existing national levels into the European structure is amenable to resolution through approximation and will necessarily be subject to further discussion but for the present purposes it is necessary to compare the general horizontal descriptors in these frameworks and explore the extent to which they can be accommodated in the prototype typology of KSCs.

For implementing the Scottish credit and qualifications framework (SCQF), a national implementation plan has been devised (SCQF, 2002), which combines HE and VET qualifications in a unitary 12 level framework; SVQs and units were mapped to this framework in 2003 (SCQF, 2003, p. 2). Each level has descriptors for learning outcomes under five broad headings:

(a) knowledge and understanding – mainly subject-based,
(b) practice (applied knowledge and understanding),
(c) generic cognitive skills, e.g. evaluation, critical analysis,
(d) communication, numeracy and IT skills,
(e) autonomy, accountability and working with others (SCQF, 2003, p. 4).

The level descriptors are of necessity general and it is important to note the caveat made by SCQF:

> These descriptors set out the characteristic generic outcomes of each level. They are intended to provide a general, shared understanding of each level and to allow broad comparisons to be made between qualifications and learning at different levels. They are not intended to give precise or comprehensive statements, and there is no expectation that every qualification or programme should have all of the characteristics (SCQF, 2003, p. 27).

The focus on learning outcomes promotes accreditation of informal and non-formal experiential learning, and a project to promote recognition of prior informal learning is underway through accreditation of prior experiential learning (APEL) (SCQF, 2004). Interestingly, nursing has been decreed a graduate-only occupation in Scotland and this has required validation of work-based learning programmes and APEL to assess and accredit the knowledge, skills and competence of nurses who trained before it was a graduate level profession.

In Ireland, the qualifications system was reformed under the *Qualifications Act 1999*, which established the National qualifications authority of Ireland (NQAI) (NFQ, 2003a). A 10-level National framework of qualifications (NFQ) has been developed in which each level is determined by a set of learning outcomes that are required to qualify for an award at that level. While learning outcomes are established international practice in VET, this approach is 'deeply alien to educationalists who fear that such an approach is inherently utilitarian, functionalist and reductionist' (Granville, 2003, p. 267). 'Learning outcomes are packages of knowledge, skill and competence' (NFQ, 2003b). Knowledge is defined as 'declarative knowledge [which] has meaning outside any specific context of application', while know-how and skill is defined as 'the goal directed performance of a task in interaction with the environment' (NFQ, 2003c, p. 21). Competence is defined as the practical application of knowledge and skill: 'the effective and creative demonstration and deployment of knowledge and skill in human situations' (NFQ, 2003c, p. 22). In the sub-strands of these three main strands of learning outcomes, competence is divided into context (which relates to the practical application of knowledge and skills), role (which relates to social competence) and learning to learn and insight (meta-competences in our typology).

Table 2: **Approaches to KSCs in EU Member States**

Country	Knowledge or cognitive competence	Skills or functional competence	Competencies or social competence	Job-based OP or universal NQF
Belgium				
Czech Republic				Professional profiles
Denmark				
Germany	*Fachkompetenz* *Sachkompetenz*	*Methodenkompetenz* *Sozialkompetenz*	*Personal-* *kompetenz*	350 OP
Estonia				
Greece				
Spain				Over 80 OP
France	*savoir (compétences théoriques)*	*savoir-faire (compétences pratiques)*	*savoir être (compétences comportementales)*	
Iceland				
Ireland	knowledge competence – context	know-how and skill	competence – role, insight and learning	NQF
Italy				
Cyprus				
Latvia				
Lithuania				
Luxembourg				
Hungary	knowledge	application of knowledge	professional attitudes and behaviour	
Malta				

Country	Knowledge or cognitive competence	Skills or functional competence	Competencies or social competence	Job-based OP or universal NQF
Netherlands	*vakmatig-methodische*		*social- communicatieve*	OP
	bestuurlijk-organisatorische en strategische		*Ontwikkelings*	
Austria	*Sachkompetenz*		*Personal-kompetenz*	
		Sozialkompetenz		
Poland				
Portugal	*competências cognitivas*	*competências funcionais*	*competências sociais*	OP; developing NQF
Slovenia				
Slovak Republic				
Finland	knowledge	working methods	core competences	Occupational fields and NQF
	safety			
Sweden				
UK: England and Wales	underpinning knowledge	functional competence	social competence	NQF under development
UK: Scotland	knowledge and understanding	practice (applied knowledge)	autonomy, accountability, working with others	NQF
	generic cognitive skills	communication, numeracy, IT skills		
UK: Northern Ireland				

Table 2 shows there is broad concordance between the countries considered to date at the level of the three dimensions associated with the KSCs typology, but the fit is not perfect. In some cases the differences can be put down largely to terminology. Thus in Ireland, the separation of competence – context (application of knowledge and skills), can be viewed as a reiteration of the idea that it is not simply knowledge and skills that matter but their application in a workplace context. This is largely implicit in the approaches of France, Portugal, Finland and England and Wales.

In several cases, the differences appear to be fundamental and conceptual. In the German model, the separation of general cognitive abilities (*Sachkompetenz*) from domain-specific knowledge and skills (*Fachkompetenz*) is paralleled in the Scottish differentiation of generic cognitive skills from knowledge and understanding appropriate for the occupation. The Scottish model also separates generic skills (communication, numeracy, IT) from what is essentially domain-specific practice.

However, in the German model, the further breaking out of specific processes (*Methodenkompetenz*) and behaviours (*Sozialkompetenz* relating both to social competence and appropriate functional behaviour), is more difficult to reconcile with other approaches, even if it reflects better the reality of the unity of work.

7.4. Occupational frameworks of KSCs

Initially, it was intended to examine competence and qualifications frameworks in a 'sunset industry' (steel or clothing); a high knowledge-based sector (pharmaceuticals or ICT); a strategic manufacturing industry (engineering or aerospace); a service sector (health); and a transversal occupational group (managers). This proved overambitious with the time and resources available and we have only been able to explore using the prototype typology tentatively against ICT occupations.

ICT occupations are interesting because they have developed without the rigidities associated with the sort of regulation that applies to health professions and the traditions of older crafts; every area of economic activity is affected by ICT and the pace of technological change makes these the most dynamic of occupations. Hence there has been neither a commonly agreed classification of ICT jobs nor an elaboration of the necessary KSCs associated with them. Noting that the trend of increasing pervasiveness of ICT shows little sign of slowing down, Petersen et al. (2004) estimate the current number of ICT workers in Europe to be approximately 3.7 million, 40 % of whom are employed in the ICT sector and 60 % in ICT user sectors (a similar breakdown is noted in the US). Clearly, therefore, ICT occupations should be a priority for action in ECVET.

The strategic importance of ICT occupations in the European economy and the highly global character of the ICT sector have resulted in substantial efforts to develop a comprehensive framework of ICT skills. In the United Kingdom, for example, key bodies in ICT, the British computer society, e-skills UK (the Sector Skills Council for ICT), the Institution of electrical engineers and the Institute for the management of information systems, formed the SFIA foundation to develop the skills framework for the information age (SFIA). The SFIA is designed to enable organisations to map existing skills and identify skills gaps and provide a framework for recruitment, training, assessment and human resource planning.

The SFIA has been created using the sort of matrix proposed for ECVET, with vertical reference levels relating to levels of responsibility and a horizontal dimension of descriptors relating to areas of work and the range of skills needed to undertake the activities. The seven levels correspond well with levels 2-8 in the reference levels agreed for ECVET but the descriptors are areas of activity or tasks (such as systems development management) rather than comprehensive descriptions of the KSCs involved, although the SFIA literature does note that the SFIA 'can be mapped to detailed competency descriptions' (SFIA, 2004). In any case, the limited user license arrangements relating to SFIA would not allow using the framework in the context of this report so no attempt is made to populate the prototype typology with the SFIA.

Career Space has undertaken mapping exercises of ICT qualifications and occupations, but this is also not amenable to incorporation into the typology without further elaboration of KSCs being fundamental to the activities described. Plant and Hammond (2004) developed a typology of cognitive abilities underlying basic ICT skills (CUBICTS) which could be incorporated into the prototype typology with the involvement of ICT specialists.

The most comprehensive attempt to date is that of Petersen et al. (2004) on behalf of Cedefop, who have made substantial progress towards a European ICT skills framework with five skill levels, summarising the complete European (reference) framework of ICT qualifications for all work areas and subdegree qualification levels. Their research into the qualitative ICT skill needs within a range of ICT business areas demonstrates that a new content oriented skill structure is needed to describe and define all ICT skills for each of the five skill levels. They note that because this skills structure is in the form of a matrix, it matters which approach and criteria are chosen as the basis of the content oriented skill structure.

Again, much of the technical description in the six generic ICT work areas is of activities, so for Technical Skills in 'ICT Support and Systems Service', the description is:

primarily concerns the analysis, troubleshooting and fixing of ICT infrastructure, systems and application problems. In principle this work covers a wide range of different ICT technologies and services and correspondingly the use of different soft and hardware based expert and diagnosis tools, depending on the level of service and support. To narrow the faults down to the concrete technical problem, ICT service practitioners need to communicate well with customers, users and colleagues. As part of the service and maintenance the ICT practitioners must be able to propose possibilities of optimising and upgrading existing ICT systems.

They also note, however, that 'by inducting the main contents and overall tasks within the six generic ICT work areas it becomes obvious that further skills than just ICT skills are also required'. The need for such skills depends on the type and contents of the work task, and they describe them as 'basic skills', falling into three categories:

(a) behavioural and personal skills:
flexibility, self learning, motivation and commitment, stress resistance and emotion, responsibility, managing risks, decision making, negotiation, initiative and attention, persuasiveness, professional attitude (business or technical orientation and interests);

(b) cross section and basic work and technical skills:
quality awareness, commercial and market awareness, entrepreneurship, customer orientation and relationship, company and business organisation, work and project organisation, business and work process knowledge, work safety and health protection, labour law and data privacy, environmental and resource awareness;

(c) soft and method skills:
communication and moderation, languages and culture, collaboration and interaction, teamwork and mentoring, conflict and consensus, creative and innovation, analytical and reasoning, problem analysis and solving, strategy, conception and planning, context and causal connection thinking, information handling, documentation and presentation.

This breakdown could conceivably be reconciled with the prototype typology since all of the behavioural and personal skills would appear as social competences; cross-section and basic work and technical skills are mostly functional competences with some basic cognitive competences; soft and method skills are a combination of functional and social and meta-competences. However, such a task must be undertaken by sector specialists at such time as this or another typology is adopted as the horizontal dimension of ECVET.

8. Conclusions and recommendations

The European policy context is increasingly emphasising both the need to integrate different routes to learning as part of the lifelong learning strategy and to develop a system of credit transfer for VET to promote mobility. A learning outcomes (or competence-based) approach offers the potential for both since it integrates the knowledge, skills and behaviours that have been acquired through diverse routes and makes transparent the basis of qualifications.

The challenge is to develop a consistent and coherent typology of KSCs in a context where even within countries there is apparent diversity in the approaches. Each existing approach has particular strengths and has been developed to suit the particular needs of the economy and VET context of the country concerned. There is therefore little merit in attempting to prescribe a one-size-fits-all typology that has not been developed for a specific labour market or training and education system. The mainstream UK approach has shown the value of occupationally-defined standards of functional competence and their applicability to the workplace. The approach adopted in France, Germany and Ireland shows the potential of a multi-dimensional and more analytical conception of KSCs.

This is a tentative effort to clarify terms and develop a prototype typology of KSCs, based on an analysis of current practice in countries that have made particular progress with competence in different ways. It is limited in both breadth and depth but forms a starting point for developing a comprehensive typology that will allow greater transparency and mobility. To operationalise and implement the typology, further actions are needed, remaining problems need to be addressed and further research is needed. Each of these issues is addressed below.

The actions needed to operationalise and implement the typology as the horizontal dimension of a European system of credit transfer must involve the main actors in VET. Ministries and agencies responsible for VET need to ensure the learning outcomes in national qualification frameworks can use the typology as a facilitating template to enable comparison with other countries. This is not a question of harmonisation, which would be politically unacceptable and unworkable given the different cultures and traditions of VET, but of accommodation to promote transparency. Adopting a competence typology requires flexibility to allow continuing reform and updating of existing qualifications frameworks in response to changes in the external environment. While the need for an overarching competence framework is important for inter-sector and international mobility, much of the detailed work will be at sector level, involving the social partners and sector training bodies. Since sector needs are relatively uniform across different countries, it is at this level the obstacles can and are being overcome.

The Leonardo da Vinci programme offers considerable potential, since many Leonardo projects are concerned with creating zones of mutual trust in developing new EU-wide qualifications. For example, three Austrian research institutes (3s, IBW and ÖIBF) initiated Leonardo project VQTS – Vocational qualification transfer system, creating a systematic procedure to ease international transfer of vocational qualifications (in terms of knowledge, skills and competencies) at secondary level. Arguing that qualifications obtained by VET students and apprentices should represent a common currency throughout Europe, the procedure has been developed and tested in the vocational field of Mechanical Engineering (Schmid, 2004, p. 23). By promoting transparency with learning outcomes, the competence typology is designed to offer a template to facilitate further cooperation. Annex 5 shows some of the Leonardo projects that, at first sight, appear to be working towards such a goal. Further work must be undertaken to gather the results of these projects and incorporate them within the ECVET work programme. In this way the 'top down' facilitating typology can act as a guide to ensure there is sufficient inter-sector comparability and commonality, while the 'bottom up' sector level zones of mutual trust ensure relevance to workplace needs.

Perhaps the greatest challenge is that if the objective of creating seamless lifelong learning is to be achieved, the typology of competence adopted in VET must dovetail with learning outcomes in higher education (Green, 1997; Green, Wolf and Leney, 2000; Huddleston and Unwin, 1997; Raffe, 2002; Stanton and Richardson, 1997; UVAC, 2000). The important social objective of making university entry possible for those who have done most of their learning at work must confront the elitism that, in most countries, has denied parity of esteem to VET. The extent to which vocational qualifications are located in a single national qualifications framework (NQF) with a single set of levels and common criteria varies enormously between countries (Bouder, 2003; Unwin et al., 2004). In the EU, Ireland and Scotland have made most progress in this respect, with the Scottish system enabling progression at crucial points between VET and HE (Raffe, 2003).

Conceptual problems may also be anticipated from the work completed to date, which has shown the difficulty is not simply in establishing an agreed terminology, but ensuring that a common vocabulary is underpinned by common meaning. The differences in VET systems and cultures present additional difficulties, but the typology must be sufficiently flexible to accommodate this diversity since it would be counterproductive to attempt to harmonise systems that have developed to suit different socioeconomic conditions. Where fundamental conceptual differences are apparent, as a result of the underlying theoretical models and assumptions, further work is needed to reconcile these and reach a common understanding without imposing a single approach. Another Austrian-led Leonardo project DISCO, launched in October 2004, is concerned with constructing a European thesaurus on skills and competencies, which will undoubtedly contribute to this issue.

Inevitably, further research is needed. It is necessary to extend the breadth of countries and complete the work begun to cover all 25 EU Member States to improve the basis for ECVET. There is also merit in researching practice beyond Europe, since the challenges are global rather than European. New Zealand has made most advance in bringing all qualifications into a single system (NZQA, 1992; Philips, 2003; Smithers, 1997; Strathdee, 2003; Tobias, 1999), while South Africa and other Commonwealth countries such as Australia are also moving in this direction (Donn and Davies, 2003; Young, 2003). These would merit further detailed study, as would the EU's major competing trading areas, the US and the Asian economies.

It is necessary to extend the depth of analysis, investigating competence in greater detail in specific occupations. Further work must be undertaken at sector level by sector specialists and we provide some broad indication of occupational frameworks that appear, *prima facie*, to be suitable for testing and operationalising the typology. Two of these are also of importance because the labour force displays extensive geographic mobility, including between Member States: the health sector (particularly nursing) and tourism.

Nursing is a regulated profession that has high standards of qualification, yet nursing universally suffers from shortages of qualified staff and chronic labour retention problems, which are expected to increase opportunities for mobility and hence interest in developing a European-wide typology of KSCs and associated European qualifications. An account of the competence framework used in the health sector in the United Kingdom is provided in Annex 3.

Tourism is unregulated (in terms of professions; obviously there is extensive regulation relating to health, sanitation, fire and safety) and most occupations in tourism have a low level of qualification. Tourism is equally affected by recruitment difficulties and high labour turnover, and some countries are developing qualification frameworks (Portugal) and occupational profiles (Italy) in this sector. Some interesting work is also underway on competence frameworks for hotel managers in Ireland (Brophy and Kiely, 2002).

Plant and process operation is a third occupational area also has potential for piloting the typology of KSCs (Rolfe, 2001a; 2001b). Over the past decade in the chemicals sector, for example, there has been growing emphasis on increasing the skills of process operators, by adding routine maintenance tasks and increasing knowledge and understanding of underlying chemical processes, to improve safety, reduce plant downtime and improve job satisfaction (Winterton and Winterton, 1997). A generic competence framework for plant and process operations developed in the Netherlands is shown in Annex 4.

Earlier work by Peterson et al. (2001) on mobility and the transparency of vocational qualifications in Europe focused on the healthcare, tourism and chemical sectors, suggesting these offer considerable scope for testing the typology.

Finally, there is also a need to address the rift between the rationalist approaches that predominate in VET systems and interpretative approaches that are becoming more widespread in the academic literature of education and training. While these approaches appear dichotomous and incompatible, developing a common ground that draws upon the strengths of each would be a major advance for both theory and practice and, like a European credit transfer system for VET, the ultimate beneficiaries will be those participating in learning at work.

List of abbreviations

ANPE	*Agence nationale pour l'emploi*
APEL	accreditation of prior experiential learning
BOS	*bestuurlijk-organisatorische en strategische dimensie*
CEEP	*Centre Européen de l'entreprise publique*
CUBICTS	cognitive abilities underlying basic ICT skills
ECTS	European credit transfer system [higher education]
ECVET	European credit transfer system for vocational education and training
EFTA	European Free Trade Association
EQF	European qualifications framework
ETUC	European Trade Union Confederation
EU	European Union
EHRD	European human resource development network
ETED	*emplois types en dynamique*
GPEC	*gestion prévisionnelle des emplois et des compétences*
HE	higher education
HRD	human resource development
HRM	human resource management
ICT	information and communication technology
IQT	Institute for Quality in Training
ISCED	international standard classification of education
ISCO	international standard classification of occupations
JCA	job competence assessment
KMK	*Kultus Minister Konferenz*
KSA	knowledge, skills and attitudes
KSC	knowledge, skills and competences
MCI	management charter initiative
MEDEF	*Mouvement des entreprises de France*
MSC	Manpower Services Commission
NCVQ	National Council for Vocational Qualifications [now QCA]

NFQ	national framework of qualifications
NQAI	National Qualifications Authority of Ireland
NVQ	national vocational qualification
NZQA	New Zealand Qualifications Authority
QCA	Qualifications and Curriculum Authority
ROME	*répertoire opérationnel des métiers et des emplois*
SCANS	State Commission on Achieving Necessary Skills
SCQF	Scottish credit and qualifications framework
SFIA	skills framework for the information age
SVQ	Scottish vocational qualification
TWG	technical working group
UEAPME	*Union Européenne des artisans et petits et moyens entreprises*
UFHRD	university forum for human resource development
UNICE	*Union des industries de la Communauté Européenne*
VET	vocational education and training
VQ	vocational qualification

References

Ackerman, P.L. (1987). Individual differences in skill learning: an integration of psychometric and information processing perspectives. *Psychological Bulletin*, Vol. 10, p. 3-27.

Ackerman, P.L. (1988). Components of individual differences during skill acquisition: cognitive abilities and information processing. *Journal of Experimental Psychology: General*, Vol. 117, p. 288-318.

Ackerman, P.L. (1992). Predicting individual differences in complex skill acquisition: dynamics of ability determinants. *Journal of Applied Psychology*, Vol. 77, p. 598-614.

Adams, J.A. (1987). Historical review and appraisal of research on the learning, retention and transfer of human motor skills. *Psychological Bulletin*, Vol. 101, p. 41-74.

Albanese, R. (1989). Competency-based management education. *Journal of Management Development*, Vol. 8, No 2, p. 14-20.

Allbredge, M.E.; Nilan, K.J. (2000). 3M's leadership competency model: an internally developed solution. *Human Resource Management*, Vol. 39, No 2, p. 133-145.

Amadieu, J.F.; Cadin, L. (1996). *Compétences et organisation qualifiante*. Paris: Economica.

Anderson, J.R. (ed.) (1981). *Cognitive skills and their acquisition*. Hilldale, NJ: Lawrence Erlbaum.

Anderson, J.R. (1982). Acquisition of cognitive skill. *Psychological Review*, Vol. 89, No 4, p. 369-406.

Anderson, J.R. (1983). *The architecture of cognition*, Cambridge, MA: Harvard University Press.

Anderson, J.R. (1987). Skill acquisition: compilation of weak-method problem solutions. *Psychological Review*, Vol. 94, p. 192-210.

Anold, R.; Nolda, S.; Nuissl, E. (2001). *Wörterbuch Erwachsenen-Pädagogik*. Bad Heilbrunn: Kilnkhardt.

Antonacopoulou, E.P.; FitzGerald, L. (1996). *Reframing competency in management development.* Human Resource Management Journal, Vol. 6, No 1, p. 27-48.

Aragon, S.R.; Johnson, S.D. (2002). Emerging roles and competencies for training in e-learning environments. *Advances in Developing Human Resources*, Vol. 4, No 4, p. 424-439.

Archan, S.; Tutschek, E. (2002). *Schlüsselqualifikationen: Wie vermittle ich sie Lehrlingen?* Vienna: Institut für Bildungsforschung der Wirtschaft.

Argyris, C.; Schön, D.A. (1974). *Theory in practice: increasing professional effectiveness*. London: Josey-Bass.

Argyris, C.; Schön, D.A. (1978). *Organisational learning*. Reading MA: Addison-Wesley.

Arnaud, G.; Lauriol, J. (2002). L'avènement du modèle de la compétence: Quelles évolutions pour la GRH? *La revue des Sciences de Gestion,* Vol. 194, p. 11-20.

Ashworth, P.; Saxton, J. (1991). On competence. *Journal of Further and Higher Education*, Vol. 14, p. 1-15.

Athey, T.R.; Orth, M.S. (1999). *Emerging competency methods for the future.* Human Resource Management, Vol. 38, No 3, p. 215-226.

Attewell, P. (1990). What is skill? *Work and occupations*, Vol. 4, p. 422-448.

Baker, D.E., Walsh, M.B.; Marjerison, L. (2000). Developing high performance leadership at the process level. *Advances in Developing Human Resources*, Vol. 6, p. 47- 72.

Bal, S. (1995). *The interactive manager*. London: Kogan Page.

Barnett, R. (1994). *Limits of competence: knowledge, higher education and society*, London: Open University Press.

Barney, J. (1991). Firm resources and sustained competitive advantage. *Journal of Management*, Vol. 17, p. 99-120.

Barney, J. (1995). Looking inside for competitive advantage. *The Academy of Management Executive*, Vol. 9, No 4, p. 49-61.

Barrett, G.V.; Depinet, R.L. (1991). A reconsideration of testing for competence rather than for intelligence. *American Psychologist*, Vol. 46, No 10, p. 1012-1024.

Barrick, M.R.; Mount, M.K. (1991). The big five personality dimensions and job performance: a meta-analysis. *Personnel Psychology*, Vol. 44, p. 1-26.

Bartlett, F. (1958). *Thinking: an experimental and social study*. New York: Basic Books.

Bataille, F. (2001). Compétence collective et performance. *Revue de Gestion des Ressources Humaines*, Vol. 40, May-June.

Bates, I. (1995). The competence movement; conceptualising recent research. *Studies in Science Education*, Vol. 25, p. 39-68.

Bateson, G. (1973). *Steps to an ecology of mind*. New York: Ballantine Books.

Beaumont, G. (1996). *Review of 100 NVQs and SVQs*. Sheffield: Department for Education and Employment.

Bell, J.; Dale, M. (1999). *Informal learning in the workplace.* Sheffield: Department for Education and Employment. (Research Report, 134).

Bellier, S. (2004). *Le savoir-être dans l'entreprise: Utilité en gestion des ressources humaines*. Paris: Vuibert.

Benner, P. (1984). *From novice to expert: excellence and power in clinical nursing practice.* San Francisco: Addison-Wesley.

Bergenhenegouwen, G.J.; ten Horn, H.F.K.; Mooijman, E.A.M. (1996). Competence development – a challenge for HRM professionals: core competences of organisations as guidelines for the development of employees. *Journal of European Industrial Training*, Vol. 20, No 9, p. 29-35.

Berry, D.C.; Broadbent, D.E. (1984). On the relationship between task-performance and associated verbalized knowledge. *Quarterly Journal of Experimental Psychology*, Vol. 36a, p. 209-231.

Billett, S. (1993). Authenticity and a culture of work practice. *Australia and New Zealand Journal of Vocational Education Research*, Vol. 2, No 1, p. 1-29.

Billett, S. (2000) Performance at work: identifying smart work practice. In Gerber, R.; Lankshear, C. (eds). *Training for a smart workforce*. London: Routledge, p. 123-150.

Bjørnåvold, J. (1997). *Identification and validation of prior and non-formal learning: experiences, innovations and dilemmas*. Luxembourg: Office for Official Publications of the European Communities.

Bjørnåvold, J. (1999). *Identification, assessment and recognition of non-formal learning: European tendencies*. In Fries Guggenheim, E. (ed.) AGORA V: identification, evaluation and recognition of non-formal learning. Luxembourg: Office for Official Publications of the European Communities. (Cedefop Reference series).

Bjørnåvold, J. (2000). *Making learning visible: identification, assessment and recognition of non-formal learning in Europe*. Luxembourg: Office for Official Publications of the European Communities. (Cedefop Reference series).

Bjørnåvold, J.; Tissot, P. (2000). Glossary. In Bjørnåvold, J. *Making learning visible: identification, assessment and recognition of non-formal learning in Europe*, p. 199-221.

Bloom, B.S. (1976). *Human characteristics and school learning*. New York: McGraw-Hill.

Bloom, B.S.; Hastings, J.T.; Madaus, G.F. (1971). *Handbook on formative and summative evaluation of student learning*. New York: McGraw Hill.

Bloom, B.S.; Mesia, B.B.; Krathwohl, D.R. (1964). *Taxonomy of educational objectives*: Vol. 1: *the affective domain*; Vol. 2: *the cognitive domain*). New York: David McKay.

Boak, G. (1991). *Developing managerial competences: the management learning contract approach*. London: Pitman.

Boam, R.; Sparrow, P. (eds) (1992). *Designing and achieving competency*. London: McGraw-Hill.

Bologna working group on qualifications frameworks (2004). *A framework for qualifications of the European higher education area*. Available from

Internet: http://www.bologna-bergen2005.no/B/Board_Meetings/050125_Brussels/BFUGB6_6a.pdf [cited 3.10.2005].

Boon, J.; van der Klink, M. (2002). Competencies: the triumph of a fuzzy concept. *Academy of Human Resource Development annual conference: proceedings*, Vol. 1, p. 327-334.

Boreham, N. (2002). Work process knowledge, curriculum control and the work-based route to vocational qualifications. *The British Journal of Educational Studies*, Vol. 50, No 2, p. 225-237.

Bouder, A. (2003). Qualifications in France: towards a national framework. *Journal of Education and Work,* Vol. 16, No 3, p. 347-356.

Boudreaux, G. (1997). Director competencies for the 21st Century: a guide for the new members of the board. *Management Quarterly*, Vol. 37 No 4, p. 32-40.

Boyatzis, R.E. (1982). *The competent manager: a model for effective performance*. New York: Wiley.

Brochier, D. (ed.) (2002). *La gestion des Compétences: Acteurs et pratiques*. Paris: Economica.

Brochier, D., Oiry, E. (2003). Dix ans de rémunération par les compétences à l'usine des plastiques: de la dynamique des acteurs à la dynamique de l'outil? In Klarsfeld, A.; Oiry, E. (eds). *Gérer les compétences: des instruments aux processus*. Paris: Vuibert, p. 59-88.

Brophy, M.; Kiely, T. (2002). Competencies: a new sector. *Journal of European Industrial Training*, Vol. 26, No 2/3/4, p. 165-176.

Brown, R.B. (1993). Meta-competence: a recipe for reframing the competence debate. *Personnel Review*, Vol. 22, No 6, p. 25-36.

Brown, R.B. (1994). Reframing the competency debate: management knowledge and meta-competence in graduate education. *Management Learning*, Vol. 25, No 2, p. 289-99.

Bryan, W.L.; Harter, N. (1897). Studies in the physiology and psychology of the telegraphic language. *Psychological Review*, Vol. 4, p. 27-53.

Bryan, W.L.; Harter, N. (1899). Studies on the telegraphic language: the acquisition of a hierarchy of habits. *Quarterly Journal of Experimental Psychology*, Vol. 10, p. 113-129.

Burgoyne, J. (1988a). *Competency based approaches to management development*. Lancaster: Centre for the Study of Management Learning.

Burgoyne, J. (1988b). Management development for the individual and the organisation. *Personnel Management*, June, p. 40-44.

Burgoyne, J. (1989a). *Management development: context and strategies*. Aldershot: Gower.

Burgoyne, J. (1989b). Creating the managerial portfolio: building on competency approaches management development. *Management Education and Development*, Vol. 20, No 1, p. 56-61.

Burgoyne, J. (1993). The competence movement: issues, stakeholders and prospects. *Personnel Review*, Vol. 22, No 6, p. 6-13.

Burgoyne, J.; Stewart, R. (1976). The nature, use and acquisition of managerial skills and other attributes. *Personnel Review*, Vol. 5, No 4, p. 19-29.

Campbell, A.; Sommers Luchs, K.S. (1997). *Core competency-based strategy*. London: Thomson.

Cannac, Y. et la CEGOS (1985). *La Bataille des compétences: l'éducation professionnelle permanent au cœur des stratégies de l'entreprise*. Paris: Editions Hommes et Techniques.

Canning, R. (1990). The quest for competence. *Industrial and commercial training*, Vol. 122, No 5, p. 12-16.

Canning, R. (2000). The rhetoric and reality of professional competence-based vocational education in Scotland. *Research Papers in Education*, Vol. 15, No 1, p. 69-93.

Cappelli, P.; Crocker-Hefter, A. (1996). Distinctive human resources are firms' core competencies. *Organisational Dynamics*, Vol. 24, No 3, p. 6-22.

Carlson, R.A., Khoo, B.H., Yaure, R.G.; Schneider, W. (1990). Acquisition of a problem-solving skill: levels of organisation and use of working memory. *Journal of Experimental Psychology: General*, Vol. 119, p. 193-214.

Carlson, R.A., Sullivan, M.A.; Schneider, W. (1989). Practice and working memory effects in building procedural skill. *Journal of Experimental Psychology: Learning, Memory and Cognition*, Vol. 15, p. 517-526.

Carlson, R.A.; Yaure, R.G. (1990). Practice schedules and the use of component skills in problem solving. *Journal of Experimental Psychology: Learning, Memory and Cognition*, Vol. 16, p. 484-496.

Carrington, L. (1994). Competent to manage? *International Management*, Vol. 49, No 7, p. 17.

Carroll, J.B. (1993). *Human cognitive abilities: a survey of factor-analytic studies*. Cambridge: Cambridge University Press.

Cazal, D.; Dietrich, A. (2003). Compétences et savoirs: quels concepts pour quelles instumentations. In Klarsfeld A.; Oiry, E. (eds). *Gérer les compétences: des instruments aux processus*. Paris: Vuibert, p. 241-262.

Chase, W.G.; Ericsson, K.A. (1982). Skill and working memory. In Bower, G.H. (ed.). *The psychology of learning and motivation*. New York: Academic Press, p. 1-58.

Cheetham, G.; Chivers, G. (1996). Towards a holistic model of professional competence. *Journal of European Industrial Training*, Vol. 20, No 5, p. 20-30.

Cheetham, G.; Chivers, G. (1998). The reflective (and competent) practitioner: a model of professional competence which seeks to harmonise the reflective practitioner and competence-based approaches. *Journal of European Industrial Training*, Vol. 22, No 7, p. 267-276.

Chi, M.T.H.; Glaser, R.; Farr, M.J. (eds) (1988). *The nature of expertise*. Hillsdale, NJ: Lawrence Erlbaum.

Chomsky, N. (1980). Rules and representations. *The Behavioural and Brain Sciences*, Vol. 3, p. 1-61.

Cockerill, T. (1989). The kind of competence for rapid change. *Personnel Management*, Vol. 21, No 9, p. 52-56.

Coffield, F. (ed.) (2000). *The necessity of informal learning*. Bristol: Policy Press.

Coles, M.; Oates, T. (2004). *European reference levels for education and training: promoting credit transfer and mutual trust*. Luxembourg: Office for Official Publications of the European Communities. (Cedefop Panorama series, 109). Available from Internet: http://www2.trainingvillage.gr/etv/publication/download/panorama/ 5146_en.pdf [cited 3.10.2005].

Colley, A.M.; Beech, J.R. (eds) (1989). *Acquisition and performance of cognitive skills*. Chichester: Wiley.

Collin, A. (1989). Managers' competence: rhetoric, reality and research. *Personnel Review*, Vol. 18, No 6, p. 20-25.

Collin, A. (1997). Learning and development. In Beardwell, I.; Holden, L. (eds). *Human resource management: a contemporary perspective*. 2nd ed. London: Pitman, p. 282-344.

Collins, D.B., Lowe, J.S.; Arnett, C.R. (2000). High-performance leadership at the organisation level. *Advances in Developing Human Resources*, Vol. 6, p. 18-46.

COLO (2003). *Format Beroepscompetentieprofiel: handleiding voor het opstellen van beroepscompetentieprofielen*. Zoetermeer: COLO.

Constable, C.J. (1988). *Developing the competent manager in a UK context*. Sheffield: Manpower Services Commission.

Cooper, K.C. (2000). *Effective competency modeling and reporting: a step-by-step guide for improving individual and organizational performance*. New York: Amacom.

Council of the European Union (2000). *Lisbon European Council: Presidency conclusions*. Brussels: Council of the European Union. Available from Internet: http://ue.eu.int/ueDocs/cms_Data/docs/pressData/en/ec/00100-r1.en0.htm [cited 3.10.2005].

Cox, J.W. (1934). *Manual skill: its organisation and development*. Cambridge: Cambridge University Press.

Crossman, E.R.F.W. (1959). A theory of the acquisition of speed-skill. *Ergonomics*, Vol. 2, p. 153-166.

Cseh, M. (2003). Facilitating learning in multicultural teams. *Advances in Developing Human Resources*, Vol. 5, No 1, p. 26-40.

Cullen, J. et al. (2000). *Informal learning and widening participation*. Sheffield: DfEE. (Research Report, 191).

Dale, M.; Iles, P. (1992). *Assessing management skills*. London: Kogan Page [1996 ed.].

Dall'Alba, G.; Sandberg, J. (1996). Educating for competence in professional practice. *Instructional Science*, Vol. 24, p. 411-437.

Daniels, D.R.; Erickson, M.L.; Dalik, A. (2001). Here to stay: taking competencies to the next level. *Work at Work Journal*, Vol. 10, No 1, p. 70-77.

Debling, G. (1991). Developing standards. In Raggatt P.; Unwin, L. (eds). *Change and intervention: vocational education and training*. London: Falmer Press.

Defélix, C., Martin, D.; Retour, D. (2001). La Gestion des Compétences entre concepts et applications. *Revue de Gestion des Ressources Humaines*, Vol. 39, p. 73-79.

Dejoux, C. (1999). Organisation qualifiante et maturité en gestion des compétences. *Direction et Gestion des Entreprises*, p. 158.

Delamare Le Deist, F.; Winterton, J. (2004). What is competence and does it matter? *Fifth Conference on HRD Research and Practice: International Comparative and Cross Cultural Dimensions of HRD*, Limerick, 27-28 May.

Delamare Le Deist, F.; Winterton, J. (2005). What is competence? *Human Resource Development International*, Vol. 8, No 1, p. 17-36.

Dietrich, A. (2003). La gestion des compétences: essai de modélisation. In Klarsfeld, A.; Oiry, E. (eds) *Gérer les compétences: des instruments aux processus*. Paris: Vuibert, p. 215-240.

Dodgson, M. (1993). Organisational learning: a review of some literature. *Organisational Studies*, Vol. 14, p. 375-394.

Donn, G.; Davies, T. (2003). *National qualification frameworks in the Commonwealth*. London: Commonwealth Secretariat.

Donnelly, E. (1991). Management charter initiative: a critique. *Training and Development*, April, p. 43-5.

Dooley, K.E. et al. (2004). Behaviourally anchored competencies: evaluation tool for training via distance. *Human Resource Development International*, Vol. 7, No 3, p. 315-332.

Dooley, L.M. et al. (2001). Differences in priority for competencies trained between U.S. and Mexican trainers. *Academy of Human Resource Development Annual Conference: proceedings*, Vol. 1, p. 115-122.

Dousset, A. (1990). *Entreprises, développez vos compétences*. Paris: Editions Entente.

Dreyfus, H.L.; Dreyfus, S.E. (1986). *Mind over machine: the power of human intuition and expertise in the era of the computer*. New York: Free Press.

Dubois, D.A.; Rothwell, W.J. (2004). *Competency-based human resource management*. Palo-Alto, CA: Davies-Black.

Dulewicz, V. (1989). Assessment centres as the route to competence. *Personnel Management*, November, p. 56-59.

Dulewicz, V.; Herbert, P. (1992). *Personality, competences, leadership style and managerial effectiveness*. Henley: Henley Management College. (Henley Working Paper, 14).

Dupray, A.; Guitton, C.; Manchatre, S. (eds) (2003). *Réfléchir la compétence: Approches sociologiques, juridiques, économiques d'une pratique gestionnaire*. Toulouse: Octarès Editions.

Durand, J.P. (2000). Les enjeux de la logique compétences. *Gérer et comprendre*, Vol. 62, décembre, p. 16-24.

Durand, T. (2000). L'alchimie de la compétence. *Revue française de gestion*, Vol. 26, January-February, p. 84-102.

Earley, P.C.; Ang, S. (2003). *Cultural intelligence: individual interactions across cultures*. Stanford: Stanford University Press.

Ecclestone, K. (1999). Empowering or ensnaring? The implications of outcome-based assessment in higher education. *Higher Education Quarterly*, Vol. 53, No 1, p. 29-48.

Ecclestone, K. (2000) Bewitched, bothered and bewildered: a policy analysis of the GNVQ assessment regime 1992-2000. *Journal of Education Policy*, Vol. 15, No 5, p. 539-558.

Elbers, E. (1991). The development of competence and its social context. *Educational Psychology Review*, Vol. 3, p. 73-94.

Elkin, G. (1990). Competency-based human resource development. *Industrial and Commercial Training*, Vol. 22, No 4, p. 20-25.

Elleström, P-E. (1992). *Kompetens, utbildning och lärande i arbetslivet: problem, begrepp och teoretiska perspektiv*. Stockholm: Publica.

Elleström, P-E. (1997). The many meanings of occupational competence and qualification. *Journal of European Industrial Training*, Vol. 21, No 6/7, p. 266-273.

Employment Department; NCVQ (1991). *Guide to national vocational qualifications*. Sheffield: Employment Department.

Engle, A.D. et al. (2001). Conceptualizing the global competency cube: a transnational model of human resource. *Journal of European Industrial Training*, Vol. 25, No 7, p. 346-353.

Eraut, M. (1994). *Developing professional knowledge and competence*. London: Falmer Press.

Eraut, M. (2000a). Non-formal learning and tacit knowledge in professional work. *British Journal of Educational Psychology*, Vol. 70, p. 113-136.

Eraut, M. (2000b). Non-formal learning, implicit learning and tacit knowledge in professional work. In Coffield, F. (ed.). *The necessity of informal learning*. Bristol: Policy Press.

Eraut, M. et al. (1998). *Development of knowledge and skills in employment.* Falmer: University of Sussex. (Institute of Education Research Report, 5).

Ericsson, K.A.; Krampe, R.T.; Tesch-Römer, C. (1993). The role of deliberate practice in the acquisition of expert performance. *Psychological Review*, Vol. 100, p. 363-406.

Ericsson, K.A.; Smith, J. (1991). Prospects and limits of the empirical study of expertise: an introduction. In Ericsson, K.A.; Smith, J. (eds). *Towards a general theory of expertise: prospects and limits.* Cambridge: Cambridge University Press, p. 1-38.

Ertl, H. (2002). The concept of modularisation in vocational education and training: the debate in Germany and its implications. *Oxford Review of Education*, Vol. 28, No 1, p. 53-73.

Estellat, N. (2003). L'appréciation des compétences ou la mise en abyme des paradoxes managériaux. In Klarsfeld, A.; Oiry, E. (eds). *Gérer les compétences: des instruments aux processus.* Paris: Vuibert, p. 107-128.

ETUC; UNICE/UEAPME; CEEP (2002). *Framework of actions for the lifelong development of competencies and qualifications.* Brussels: ETUC, UNICE/ UEAPME, CEEP. Available from Internet: http://www.etuc.org/a/580 [cited 3.10.2005].

European Commission (2000). *A memorandum on lifelong learning.* Brussels: Commission of the European Communities. (SEC(2000) 1832). Available from Internet: http://www.bologna-berlin2003.de/pdf/MemorandumEng. pdf [cited 3.10.2005].

European Commission (2001a). *Making a European area of lifelong learning a reality.* Brussels: Commission of the European Communities. Available from Internet: http://europa.eu.int/comm/education/policies/lll/life/ communication/com_en.pdf [cited 3.10.2005].

European Commission (2001b). *High-level task force on skills and mobility: final report.* Available from Internet: http://europa.eu.int/comm/employment_ social/ publications/2001/ke4302082_en.pdf [cited 3.10.2005].

European Commission (2004). *Towards a European framework (and a credit transfer system for VET).* 3 December [Policy document presented to the Education Council].

Evers, F.T.; Berdrow, I.; Rush, J.C. (1998). *The bases of competence: skills for lifelong learning and employability.* New York: Jossey Bass Wiley.

Field, J. (1991). Competency and the pedagogy of labour. *Studies in the Education of Adults*, Vol. 23, No 1, p. 41-51.

Field, J. (1995). Reality testing in the workplace: are NVQs 'employment-led'? In Hodkinson P.; Issitt, M. (eds). *The challenge of competence.* London: Cassell Education.

Field, J. (ed.) (2002). *Promoting European dimensions in lifelong learning.* Leicester: National Institute of Adult Continuing Education.

Fielding, N.G. (1998a). Competence and culture in the police. *Sociology*, Vol. 22, p. 45-64.

Fielding, N.G. (1998b). *Joining forces: police training, socialization and occupational competence*. London: Routledge.

Finn, R. (1993). *A synthesis of current research on management competences*. Henley: Henley Management College. (Henley Working Paper, 10).

Fischer, K.W. et al. (1993). The dynamics of competence: how context contributes directly to skill. In Wozniak, R.H.; Fischer, K.W. (eds). *Development in context: acting and thinking in specific environments*. Hillsdale, NJ: Erlbaum, p. 93-117.

Fitts, P.M.; Bahrick, H.P.; Noble, M.E.; Briggs, G.E. (1961). *Skilled performance*. New York: John Wiley.

Fitts, P.M.; Posner, M.I. (1967). *Human performance*. Belmont, CA: Brooks/ Cole.

Flanagan, M., McGinn, I.; Thornhill, A. (1993). *Because no bastard ever asked me*. Canberra: Stakeholder.

Fleishman, E.A.; Quaintance, M.K. (1984). *Taxonomies of human performance: the description of human tasks*. Orlando, FL: Academic Press.

Foss, N.J.; Knudsen, C. (eds) (1996). *Towards a competence theory of the firm*. London: Routledge.

Fowler, E. (1994). In search of the best standards. *Personnel Today*, 22 March, p. 15.

Foxan, M.J. (1998). Closing the global leadership competency gap: the Motorola GOLD Process. *Organisation Development Journal*, Vol. 16, p. 5-12.

Frank, E. (1991). The United Kingdom's management charter initiative: the first three years. *Journal of European Industrial Training*, Vol. 17, No 1, p. 9-11.

Fuchs, A.H. (1962). The progression-regression hypothesis in perceptual-motor skill learning. *Journal of Experimental Psychology*, Vol. 63, p. 177-182.

Fuller, A. (1995). Purpose value and competence: contextualising competence-based assessment in the civil aviation sector. *Journal of Education and Work*, Vol. 8, No 2, p. 60-77.

Gagné, R.M. (1962). The acquisition of knowledge. *Psychological Review*, Vol. 69, p. 355-365.

Gagné, R.M.; Foster, H.; Crowley, M.E. (1948). Measurement of transfer of training. *Psychological Bulletin*, Vol. 45, p. 97-130.

Gangani, N.T.; McLean, G.N.; Braden, R.A. (2004). Competency-based human resource development strategy. *Academy of Human Resource Development Annual Conference: proceedings*, Vol. 2, p. 1111-1118.

Gangloff, B. (2000). *Les compétences professionnelles*. Paris: L'Harmattan.

Garvin, D. (1993). Building a learning organisation. *Harvard Business Review*, Vol. 71, No 4, p. 78-91.

Gelman, R.; Greeno, J.G. (1989). On the nature of competence. Principles for understanding in a domain. In Resnick, L.B. (ed.). *Knowing, learning and instruction*. Hillsdale, NJ: Erlbaum, p. 125-186.

Gerber, R. (2000). Experience, common sense and expertise in workplace learning. In Gerber R.; Lankshear, C. (eds). *Training for a smart workforce*. London: Routledge, p. 73-96.

Gerber, R; Lankshear, C. (2000). Introduction. In Gerber, R. and Lankshear, C. (eds). *Training for a smart workforce*. London: Routledge, p. 1-9.

Gerber, R.; Velde, C.R. (1996). Clerical-adminstrative workers' conceptions of competence in their jobs. *Vocational Aspect of Education*, Vol. 48, p. 393-403.

Gilbert, P. (1998). *L'évaluation des compétences à l'épreuve des faits*. Luxembourg: Entreprise et Personnel.

Gilbert, P. (2003). Jalons pour une histoire de la gestion des compétences. In Klarsfeld, A.; Oiry, E. (eds). *Gérer les compétences: des instruments aux processus*. Paris: Vuibert, p. 11-32.

Glaser, R. (1984). Education and thinking: the role of knowledge. *American Psychologist*, Vol. 39, No 2, p. 93-104.

Goleman, D. (1995). *Emotional intelligence: why it can matter more than IQ?* New York: Bantam Books.

Gonczi, A. (1994). *Developing a competent workforce*. Adelaide: National Centre for Vocational Education Research.

Grant, G. et al. (1979). *On competence: a critical analysis of competence-based reforms in higher education*. San Francisco: Jossey-Bass.

Grant, R.M. (1991). The resource-based theory of competitive advantage: implications for strategy formulation. *California Management Review*, Vol. 33, No 3, p. 114-22.

Granville, G. (2003). 'Stop making sense': chaos and coherence in the formulation of the Irish qualifications framework. *Journal of Education and Work*, Vol. 16, No 3, p. 259-270.

Green, A. (1997). Core skills, general education and unification. In Hodgson, A.; Spours, K. (eds). *Daring and beyond*. London: Kogan Page.

Green, A., Wolf, A.; Leney, T. (2000). *Convergence and divergence in English education and training systems*. London: Institute of Education.

Green, P. C. (1999). *Building robust competencies*. San Francisco, CA: Jossey-Bass.

Greeno, J.G.; Riley, M.S.; Gelman, R. (1984). Conceptual competence and children's counting. *Cognitive Psychology*, Vol. 16, p. 94-143.

Guion, R.M. (1991). *Personnel assessment, selection and placement*. Palo Alto, CA: Consulting Psychological Press.

Haddadj, S.; Besson, D. (2000a). Introduction à la gestion des compétences. *Revue française de gestion*, Vol. 26, January-February, p. 82-83.

Haddadj, S.; Besson, D. (2000b). Gestion des compétences et relations sociales: une étude de cas chez Renault. *Revue française de gestion*, Vol. 26, January-February.

Hager, P. (1994). Is there a cogent philosophical argument against competency standards? *Australian Journal of Education*, Vol. 38, p. 3-18.

Hall, R. (1992). The strategic analysis of intangible resources. *Strategic Management Journal*, Vol. 13, p. 135-44.

Hamel, G.; Prahalad, C.K. (1994). *Competing for the future*. Cambridge, Mass.: Harvard Business School Press.

Hansson, B. (2001). Competency models: are self-perceptions accurate enough? *Journal of European Industrial Training*, Vol. 27, No 9, p. 428-441.

Harris, R. et al. (1995). *Competency based education and training: between a rock and a whirlpool*. South Melbourne: Macmillan Educational Australia.

Hartle, F. (1995). *How to re-engineer your performance management process*. London: Kogan Page.

Harvey, M.G.; Speier, C.; Novicevic, M.M. (2000). An innovative global management staffing system: a competency-based perspective. *Human Resource Management*, Vol. 39, No 4, p. 381-394.

Hay, J. (1990). Managerial competences or managerial characteristics? *Management Education and Development*, Vol. 21, No 4, p. 305-15.

Hay Group, Towers Perrin, Hewitt Associates Llc, M. William Mercer inc. and American Compensation Association (1996). *Raising the bar: using competencies to enhance employee performance*. Scottsdale, AZ: American Compensation Association.

Hayes, J.L. (1979). A new look at managerial competence: the AMA model of worthy performance. *Management Review*, November, p. 2-3.

Hayes, J.L. (1980a). The AMA model for superior performance: part II: how can I do a better job as a manager? *Management Review*, February, p. 2-3.

Hayes, J.L. (1980b.) The AMA model for superior performance: part III: how competent managers work with people. *Management Review*, March, p. 2-3.

Heidemann, W. et al. (1998). *Validation and recognition of competences and qualifications: European discussion paper for the social partners: final report of Leonardo da Vinci project VALID*. Düsseldorf: Hans Böckler Stiftung, Düsseldorf.

Henderson, R.; Cockburn, I. (1994). Measuring competence? Exploring the firm effects in pharmaceutical research. *Strategic Management Journal*, Vol. 15, p. 63-84.

Hendry, C.; Arthur, M.B.; Jones, A.M. (1995). *Strategy through people: adaptation and learning in the small-medium enterprise*. London: Routledge.

Hermann, G.D.; Kenyon, R.J. (1987). *Competency-based vocational education*. Further Education Unit, Falmer: University of Sussex.

Hirsh, W.; Strebler, M. (1994). Defining managerial skills and competences. In Mumford, A. (ed.). *Gower Handbook of Management Development*. Aldershot: Gower, p. 79-96.

Hitt, M.A.; Ireland, D.R. (1985). Corporate distinctive competence, strategy, industry and performance. *Strategic Management Journal*, Vol. 6, p. 273-293.

Hitt, M.A.; Ireland, D.R. (1986). Relationships among corporate level distinctive competencies, diversification strategy, corporate structure and performance. *Journal of Management Studies*, Vol. 23, p. 400-416.

Hodkinson, P.; Issitt, M. (1995). *The challenge of competence*. London: Cassell Education.

Hoffmann, T. (1999). The meanings of competency. *Journal of European Industrial Training*, Vol. 23, No 6, p. 275-285.

Holding, D.F. (ed.) (1989). *Human skills*. New York: John Wiley (2nd ed.).

Holton, E.F.; Lynham, S.A. (2000). Performance-driven leadership development. *Advances in Developing Human Resources*, Vol. 6, p. 1-17.

Huddleston, P.; Unwin, L. (1997). Stakeholders, skills and star-gazing: the problematic relationship between education, training and the labour market. In Stanton, G.; Richardson, W. (eds). *Qualifications for the future: a study of tripartite and other divisions in post-16 education and training*. London: Further Education Development Agency.

Hussey, D.E. (1988). *Management training and corporate strategy: how to improve competitive performance*. Oxford: Pergamon.

Hussey, D. (1996). *Business driven human resource management*. Chichester: Wiley.

Hyland, T. (1992). Meta-competence, metaphysics and vocational expertise. *Competence and Assessment*, No 20, Sheffield: Employment Department.

Hyland, T. (1994). *Competence, education and NVQs: dissenting perspectives*. London: Cassell Education.

Hyland, T. (1995). Behaviourism and the meaning of competence. In Hodkinson, P.; Isett, M. (eds). *The challenge of competence.* London: Cassell.

Iles, P. (1993). Achieving strategic coherence in HRD through competency-based management and organisation development. *Personnel Review*, Vol. 22, No 6, p. 63-80.

Institute of Management (1994). *Management development to the millennium: the Cannon and Taylor working party reports*. London: Institute of Management.

Investors in people UK (1995). *The investors in people standard*. London: IiP UK.

Jacobs, R. (1989). Getting the measure of management competence. *Personnel Management*, Vol. 21, No 6, p. 32-37.

Jacques, E. (1956). *Measurement of responsibility*. Falls Church, VA: Cason Hall.

Jacques, E. (1961). *Equitable payment*. Falls Church, VA: Cason Hall.

Jacques, E. (1964). *Time span handbook*. Falls Church, VA: Cason Hall.

Jacques, E. (1994). *Human capability*. Falls Church, VA: Cason Hall.

Jeris, L.; Johnson, K. (2004). Speaking of competence: toward a cross-translation for human resource development (HRD) and continuing professional education (CPE). *Academy of Human Resource Development Annual Conference: proceedings*, Vol. 2, p. 1103-1110.

Jessup, G. (1991). *Outcomes: NVQs and the emerging model of education and training*. London: Falmer Press.

Johnson, S.; Winterton, J. (1999). *Management skills*. London: Department for Education and Employment. (Skills Task Force Research Paper, 3)

Johnston, R.; Sampson, M. (1993). The acceptable face of competence. *Management education and development*, Vol. 24, No 3, p. 216-24.

Jones, L.; Moore, R. (1995). Appropriating competence: the competency movement, the New Right and the 'culture change' project. *British Journal of Education and Work*, Vol. 8, No 2, p. 78-92.

Joras, M. (2002). *Le Bilan de compétences*. 3rd ed. Paris: PUF. (*Que sais-je?*, 2979).

Jubb, R.; Rowbotham, D. (1997). Competences in management development: challenging the myths. *Journal of European Industrial Training*, Vol. 21, No 5, p. 171-175.

Kamarainen, P.; Attwell, G.; Brown, A. (eds) (2002). *Transformation of learning in education and training: key qualifications revisited*. Luxembourg: Office for Official Publications of the European Commission. (Cedefop Reference, 37).

Kanugo, R.N.; Misra, S. (1992). Managerial resourcefulness: a reconceptualisation of management skills. *Human Relations*, Vol. 45, No 12, p. 1311-1332.

Keating, D.P. (1978). A search for social intelligence. *Journal of Educational Psychology*, Vol. 70, p. 218-223.

Keep, E.; Mayhew, K. (1999). The assessment of knowledge, skills and competitiveness. *Oxford Journal of Economic Policy*, Vol. 15, No 1, p. 1-15.

Keller, F.S. (1958). The phantom plateau. *Journal of the Experimental Analysis of Behaviour*, Vol. 1, p. 1-13.

Kieras, D.E.; Bovair, S. (1984). The role of a mental model in learning to operate a device. *Cognitive Science*, Vol. 8, p. 255-273.

Kim, D.H. (1993). The link between individual and organisational learning. *Sloan Management Review*, Fall, p. 37-50.

Kilcourse, T. (1994). Developing competent managers. *Journal of European Industrial Training*, Vol. 18, No 2, p. 12-16.

Klarsfeld, A. (2000). La compétence, ses définitions, ses enjeux. *Revue Gestion 2000*, March-April, p. 31-47.

Klarsfeld, A.; Oiry, E. (eds) (2003). *Gérer les compétences: des instruments aux processus*. Paris: Vuibert.

Klarsfeld, A.; Roques, O. (2003). Histoire d'une instrumentation de gestion des compétences: entre rationalité contingente, rationalité limité et rationalité institutionelle. In Klarsfeld, A. and Oiry, E. (eds). *Gérer les compétences: des instruments aux processus*. Paris: Vuibert, p. 171-190.

Klarsfeld, A.; Saint-Onge, S. (2000). La rémunération des compétences: théorie et pratique. In Peretti, J.-M.; Roussel, P. (eds). *Les Rémunérations: Politiques et pratiques pour les années 2000*. Paris: Vuibert, p. 65-80.

Klemp, G.O. (ed.) (1980). *The assessment of occupational competence: report to the National Institute of Education*. Washington, DC: National Institute of Education.

Klemp, G.O.; Spencer, L.M. (1982). *Job competence assessment*. Reading, MA: Addison-Wesley.

Klieme, E. et al. (2004). *The development of national educational standards: an expertise*. Berlin: Bundesministerium für Bildung und Forschung.

Knasel, E.; Meed, J. (1994). *Becoming competent: effective learning for occupational competence*. Sheffield: Employment Department.

Kolb, D.A. et al. (1986). Strategic management development: using experiential learning theory to assess and develop management competencies. *Journal of Management Development*, Vol. 5, No 3, p. 13-24.

Kolb, D.A.; Rubin, I.; McIntyre, J.M. (1971). *Organisational psychology: an experiential approach*. Englewood Cliffs, NJ: Prentice Hall.

Konrad, J. (2000). Assessment and verification of National Vocational Qualifications: policy and practice. *Journal of Vocational Education and Training*, Vol. 52, No 2, p. 225-242.

Kraiger, K.; Ford, J.K.; Salas, E. (1993). Application of cognitive, skill-based and affective theories of learning outcomes to new methods of training evaluation. *Journal of Applied Psychology*, Vol. 78, No 2, p. 311-328.

Kusterer, K.C. (1978). *Know-how on the job: the important working knowledge of 'unskilled' workers*. Boulder, CO: Westview.

Lavery, J.J. (1962). Retention of simple motor skills as a function of type of knowledge of results. *Canadian Journal of Psychology*, Vol. 16, p. 300-311.

Le Boterf, G. (1994). *De la compétence: essai sur un attracteur étrange*. Paris: Editions d'Organisation.

Le Mouillour, I. (2004). *European approaches to credit (transfer) systems in VET*. Thessaloniki: Cedefop.

Leconte, P.; Forgues, B. (2000). Les dirigeants face à la gestion des compétences. *Revue française de Gestion*, Vol. 26, January-February.

Lei, D.; Hitt, M.A.; Bettis, R. (1996). Dynamic core competences through meta-learning and strategic context. *Journal of Management*, Vol. 22, p. 549-569.

Lepron, S. (2001). La démarche compétences. Outil de performance au service de la stratégie. *Revue Entreprises*, Vol. 44, May-June, p. 16-26.

Lepsinger, R. (1995). Use competency models to support organisational change. *Human Resource Professional*, Vol. 8, No 4, p. 7-10.

Lesgold, A. et al. (1988). Expertise in a complex skill: diagnosing X-ray pictures. In Chi, M.T.H.; Glaser, R.; Farr, M.J. (eds). *The nature of expertise*. Hillsdale, NJ: Lawrence Erlbaum, p. 311-342.

Lester, S. (2001). The construction of qualification levels and frameworks: issues from three UK projects. *Higher Education Quarterly*, Vol. 55, No 4, p. 396-415.

Levy-Leboyer, C. (1996). *La gestion des compétences*. Paris: Les Editions d'Organisation.

Lindsay, P.R.; Stuart, R. (1997). Reconstruing competence. *Journal of European Industrial Training*, Vol. 21, No 9, p. 326-332.

Linstead, S. (1991). Developing management meta-competence: can learning help? *Journal of European Industrial Training*, Vol. 6, No 14, p. 17-27.

Lintern, G.; Gopher, D. (1978). Adaptive training of perceptual-motor skills: issues, results and future directions. *International Journal of Man-Machine Studies*, Vol. 10, p. 521-551.

Logie, R. et al. (1989). Working memory in the acquisition of complex cognitive skills. *Acta Psychologica*, Vol. 71, p. 53-87.

Louart, P. (2003). L'impact des systèmes éducatifs sur la gestion des compétences: une comparaison internationale. In Klarsfeld, A.; Oiry, E. (eds). *Gérer les compétences: Des instruments aux processus*. Paris: Vuibert, p. 33-58.

Lucia, A.D.; Lepsinger, R. (1999). *The art and science of competency models: pinpointing critical success factors in organisations*. San Francisco: Jossey-Bass.

McBeath, G. (1990). *Practical management development: strategies for management resourcing and development in the 1990s*. Oxford: Blackwell.

McClelland, D. (1973). Testing for competence rather than for 'intelligence'. *American Psychologist*, Vol. 28, No 1, p. 1-14.

McClelland, D. (1976). *A guide to job competency assessment*. Boston: McBer & Co.

McClelland, D. (1998). Identifying competencies with behavioural-event interviews. *Psychological Science*, Vol. 9, No 5, p. 331-339.

McClelland, S. (1994). Gaining competitive advantage through strategic management development. *Journal of Management Development*, Vol. 13, No 5, p. 4-13.

McCollum, A. (2003). *Identifying the development needs of primary care workers caring for people with mild to moderate mental illness*. Edinburgh: Scottish Development Centre for Mental Health/NHS Education for Scotland.

McKeithen, K.B. (1981). Knowledge organisation and skill differences in computer programmers. *Cognitive Psychology*, Vol. 13, p. 307-325.

Mahoney, J.T.; Pandian, J.R.C. (1992). The resource based view within the conversation of strategic management. *Strategic Management Journal*, Vol. 13, p. 363-380.

Mandon, N. (1990). *La gestion prévisionnelle des compétences: la méthode ETED*. Marseille: CEREQ. (Collection des Etudes, 57).

Mandon, N. (1998). *Analyse des emploi et des compétences: la mobilisation des acteurs dans l'approche ETED*. Marseille: CEREQ. (CEREQ document, 135).

Mandon, N.; Liaroutzos, O. (eds) (1994). *La gestion des compétences: La méthode ETED en application*. Marseille: CEREQ. (CEREQ document, 97).

Mangham, I. (1986). In search of competence. *Journal of General Management*, Vol. 12, No 2, p. 5-12.

Manpower Services Commission (1986). *SASU Note 16: guidance on designing modules for accreditation*. Sheffield: Standards and Assessment Support Unit. MSC [mimeo].

Mansfield, B. (1993). Competency-based qualifications: a response. *Journal of European Industrial Training*, Vol. 17, No 3, p. 19-22.

Mansfield, B. (2004). Competence in transition. *Journal of European Industrial Training*, Vol. 28, No 2/3/4, p. 296-309.

Mansfield, B.; Mathews, D. (1985). *Job competence: a description for use in vocational education and training*. Blagdon: Further Education College.

Mansfield, B.; Mitchell, L. (1996). *Towards a competent workforce*. London: Gower.

Margerison, C. (1985). Achieving the capacity and competence to manage. *Journal of Management Development*, Vol. 4, No 3, p. 42-55.

Martin, D.P. (2003). Pour une approche compréhensive du concept de compétence: positionnement épistémologique et illustrations. In Klarsfeld, A.; Oiry, E. (eds). *Gérer les compétences: des instruments aux processus*. Paris: Vuibert, p. 263-282.

Mathewman, J. (1995). Trends and developments in the use of competency frameworks. *Competency*, Vol. 1, No 4 [special issue].

Matlay, H. (2000). S/NVQs in Britain: employer-led or ignored? *Journal of Vocational Education and Training*, Vol. 52, No 1, p. 135-148.

Mayer, E. (1992). *Employment-related key competencies for post-compulsory education and training: discussion paper.* Melbourne: Ministry of Education and Training.

MEDEF (2002). *Objectif Compétences: des pratiques Européenne innovantes.* Paris: Mouvement des Entreprises de France.

Merchiers, J.; Pharo, ·P. (1992). Eléments pour un modèle sociologique de la compétence d'expert. *Sociologie du Travail*, Vol. 34, No 1, p. 47-63.

Merle, P. (1996). *La compétence en question; école, insertion, travail.* Rennes: Presses Universitaires de Rennes.

Messick, S. (1984). The psychology of educational measurement. *Journal of Educational Measurement*, Vol. 21, p. 215-238.

Meyer, C. (2002). Transfer of concepts and practices of vocational education and training from the centre to the peripheries: the case of Germany. *Journal Education and Work*, Vol. 14, No 2, p. 189-207.

Miller, L. (1991). Managerial competences. *Industrial and Commercial Training*, Vol. 23, No 6, p. 11-15.

Minet, F. (1994). Les compétences au cœur de la gestion des ressources humaines. In Minet, F.; Parlier, M.; de Witte, S. (eds). *La compétence: mythe, construction ou réalité?* Paris: L'Harmattan, p. 11-20.

Minet, F.; Parlier, M.; de Witte, S. (eds) (1994). *La compétence: mythe, construction ou réalité?* Paris: L'Harmattan.

Mirabile, R.J. (1997). Implementation planning: key to successful competency strategies. *Human Resource Professional*, Vol. 10, No 4, p. 19-23.

Mitrani, A.; Dalziel, M.; Fitt, D. (1992). *Competency based human resource management.* London: Kogan Page.

More, C. (1980). *Skill and the English working class, 1870-1914.* London: Croom Helm.

Muller, J. (2000). *Reclaiming knowledge.* London: Falmer Press.

Murray, S. et al. (2003). *Improving out-of-hours palliative care in the community: the views of patients and their informal and professional carers.* Edinburgh: CSO/SEHD.

Nadler, D.A.; Tushman, M. (1999). The organisation of the future: strategic imperatives and core competencies for the 21st Century. *Organisational Dynamics*, Vol. 27, No 1, p. 45-58.

Naquin, S.S.; Holton, E.F. (2002). The development of a competency model and assessment instrument for public sector leadership and management development. *Academy of Human Resource Development annual conference*: proceedings, Vol. 1, p. 139-146.

Naquin, S.S.; Wilson, J. (2002). Creating competency standards, assessments and certification. *Advances in Developing Human Resources*, Vol. 4, No 2, p. 180-187.

National Framework of Qualifications (2003a). *The national framework of qualifications: an introduction*. Dublin: NFQ.

National Framework of Qualifications (2003b). *The national framework of qualifications: a brief technical guide*. Dublin: NFQ.

National Framework of Qualifications (2003c). *Policies and criteria for the establishment of the national framework of qualifications*. Dublin: NFQ.

Nelson, T.D.; Narens, L. (1990). Metamemory: a theoretical framework and new findings. *The Psychology of Learning and Motivation*, Vol. 26, p. 125-173.

NES QACPD (2003). *Caring for people with dermatological conditions: core curriculum*. Edinburgh: NHS Education for Scotland.

NES QACPD (2004). *A route to enhanced competence for nurse practitioners working in minor injury units, A&E and community hospital casualty departments*. Edinburgh: NHS Education for Scotland.

Newell, A.; Rosenbloom, P.S. (1981). Mechanisms of skill acquisition and the law of practice. In Anderson, J.R. (ed.). *Cognitive skills and their acquisition*. Hillsdale, NJ: Lawrence Erlbaum, p. 1-55.

Newell, K.M. (1991).Motor skill acquisition. *Annual Review of Psychology*, Vol. 42, p. 213-237.

NHS Education for Scotland (2004). *Out of hours: mapping and supporting new roles for practitioners in unscheduled care*. Edinburgh: NHS Education for Scotland.

NHS Quality Improvement Scotland (2004). *Draft standards for provision of safe and effective primary medical services out-of-hours*. Edinburgh: NHS QIS.

NHS24 (2003). *NHS24 Competencies for nurse advisors*. V2.0. Edinburgh: NHS24.

Nitardy, C.N.; McLean, G.N. (2002). Project management competencies needed by HRD professionals: a literature review. *Academy of Human Resource Development conference: proceedings*, Vol. 2, p. 956-963.

Nonaka, I.; Takeuchi, H. (1995). The knowledge-creating company. Oxford: Oxford University Press.

Nordhaug, O. (1993). *Human capital in organisations*. Oslo: Scandinavian University Press.

Norris, N. (1991). The trouble with competence. *Cambridge Journal of Education*, Vol. 21, No 3, p. 1-11.

Novak, J.; Gowin, D. (1984). Learning how to learn. Cambridge: Cambridge University Press.

Nursing and Midwifery Council (2002a). *Professional code of conduct*. London: NMC.

Nursing and Midwifery Council (2002b). *Higher level of practice project report*. London: NMC.

Nursing and Midwifery Council (2004). *Standards of proficiency for pre-registration nursing education*. London: NMC.

Nuthall, G. (1999). Learning how to learn: the evolution of students' minds through the social processes and culture of the classroom. *International Journal of Educational Research*, Vol. 31, No 3, p. 139-256.

Nyhan, B. (1991). *Developing people's ability to learn: a European perspective on self-learning competency and technological change*. Brussels: Eurotecnet Technical Assistance Office on behalf of the CEC.

NZQA (1992). *An introduction to the framework*. Wellington: New Zealand Qualifications Authority.

OECD (1996). *Assessing and certifying occupational skills and competencies in vocational education and training*. Paris: Organisation for Economic Cooperation and Development.

O'Neil, H.F. (ed.) (1997). *Workforce readiness: competence and assessment.* New York: Lawrence Erlbaum.

Overton, U.F. (1985). Scientific methodologies and the competence - moderator - performance issue. In Neimark, E.; Delisi, R.; Newman, J. (eds). *Moderators of competence*. Hillsdale, NJ: Erlbaum, p. 15-41.

Paraponaris, C. (2003). L'instrumentation de la gestion des compétences: une instrumentation à finalités multiples? In Klarsfeld, A.; Oiry, E. (eds). *Gérer les compétences: des instruments aux processus*. Paris: Vuibert, p. 191-214.

Parlier, M. (1994). La compétence au service d'objectifs de gestion. In Minet, F.; Parlier, M.; de Witte, S. (eds). *La compétence: mythe, construction ou réalité?* Paris: L'Harmattan, p. 91-108.

Parlier, M., Perrien, C.; Thierry D. (2000). L'organisation qualifiante et ses enjeux dix ans après. *Revue française de Gestion*, Vol. 26, p. 4-17.

Pate, J.; Martin, G.; Robertson, M. (2003). Accrediting competencies: a case of Scottish vocational qualifications. *Journal of European Industrial Training*, Vol. 27, No 2/3/4, p. 169-176.

Pear, T.H. (1927). Skill. *Journal of Personnel Research*, Vol. 5, p. 478-489.

Pear, T.H. (1948). Professor Bartlett on skill. *Occupational Psychology*, Vol. 22, p. 92-93.

Perkins, D.N.; Salomon, G. (1989). Are cognitive skills context bound? *Educational Researcher*, Vol. 18, No 1, p. 16-25.

Petersen, A.W. et al. (2004). *ICT and e-business skills and training in Europe: towards a comprehensive European e-skills reference framework*. Luxembourg: Office for Official Publications of the European Communities. (Cedefop Panorama, 93). Available from Internet: http://www2. trainingvillage.gr/etv/publication/download/ panorama/5149_en.pdf [cited 3.10.2005].

Pettersson, S. et al. (2001). *Mobility and transparency of vocational qualifications: an overview of studies in the tourism, chemical and healthcare sectors in Europe.*Luxembourg: Office for Official Publications of the European Communities. (Cedefop Panorama, 14). Available from Internet: http:// libserver.cedefop.eu.int/ vetelib/eu/pub/cedefop/pan/2001_5120_en.pdf [cited 3.10.2005].

Pettersson, S. (2004). *ECVET models, core elements and pitfalls in conceptual work.* ECVET TWG document, 11 March.

Philips, D. (2003). Lessons from New Zealand's national qualifications framework. *Journal of Education and Work*, Vol. 16, No 3, p. 289-304.

Piaget, J. (1947). *La psychologie de l'intelligence.* Paris: Colin.

Piskurich, G.M.; Saunders, E.S. (1998). *ASTD models for learning technologies: roles, competencies and outputs.* Alexandria, VA: American Society for Training and Development.

Plant, R.R.; Hammond, N. (2004). *CUBICTS Cognitive abilities underlying basic ICT skills.* York: LTSN Psychology, University of York.

Pochet, C. (1999). Productivité et sciences de gestion. *Problèmes Economiques*, No 2629, September, p. 27-32.

Polanyi, M. (1967). *The tacit dimension.* London: Routledge/Kegan Paul.

Pottinger, P.S.; Goldsmith, J. (eds) (1979). *Defining and measuring competence.* San Francisco, CA: Jossey-Bass.

Prahalad, C.K.; Hamel, G. (1990). The core competence of the corporation. *Harvard Business Review*, May-June, p. 79-91.

Proctor, R.W.; Dutta, A. (1995). *Skill acquisition and human performance.* London: Sage.

Purcell, J. (2001). National vocational qualifications and competence-based assessment for technicians: from sound principles to dogma. *Education and Training*, Vol. 43, No 1, p. 30-39.

Quélin, B.; Arrègle, J.-L. (2000). *Le management stratégique des compétences.* Paris: Edition Ellipses.

Quinn, J.B.; Anderson, P.; Finkelstein, S. (1996). Leveraging intellect. *The Academy of Management Executive*, Vol. 10, No 3, p. 7-27.

Raffe, D. (2002). *Bringing academic education and vocational training closer together.* Edinburgh: University of Edinburgh. (Centre for Educational Sociology Working Paper, 5)

Raffe, D. (2003). 'Simplicity itself': the Scottish credit and qualifications framework. *Journal of Education and Work*, Vol. 16, No 3, p. 239-257.

Raoult, N. (1991). *Gestion prévisionnelle des emplois et des compétences en milieu hospitalier.* Paris: L'Harmattan.

Raven, J. (1984). *Competence in modern society.* Edinburgh: Dinwiddie Grieve.

Rees, B.A. (2003). *The construction of management: competence and gender issues at work*. London: Edward Elgar.

Reilly, P. (ed.) (2003). *New reward I: team, skill and competence-based pay*. Brighton: Institute of Employment Studies.

Reynolds, M.; Snell, R. (1988). *Contribution to development of management competence*. Sheffield: Manpower Services Commission.

Robinson, P (1996). *Rhetoric and reality: Britain's new vocational qualifications*. London: Centre for Economic Performance.

Robotham, D.; Jubb, R. (1996). Competences: measuring the unmeasurable. *Management Development Review*, Vol. 9, No 5, p. 25-29.

Rodgriguez, D. et al. (2002). Developing competency model to promote integrated human resource practices. *Human Resource Management*, Vol. 41, p. 309-324.

Rolfe, H. (2001a). Mobility in the European chemicals industry sector: the role of transparency and recognition of vocational qualifications. Luxembourg: Office for Official Publications of the European Communities. (Cedefop Panorama, 2). Available from Internet: http://libserver.cedefop.eu.int/ vetelib/eu/pub/cedefop/pan/2001_ 5109_en.pdf [cited 3.10.2005].

Rolfe, H. (2001b). Qualifications and international mobility: a case study of the European chemicals industry. *National Institute Economic Review*, Vol. 175, No 1, p. 85-94.

Rothwell, W.J.; Lindholm, J.E. (1999). Competency identification, modeling and assessment in the USA. *International Journal of Training and Development*, Vol. 3, No 2, p. 90-105.

Russ-Eft, D. (1995). Defining competencies: a critique. *Human Resource Development Quarterly*, Vol. 6, No 4, p. 329-335.

Rutherford, P. (1995). *Competency based assessment.* Melbourne: Pitman.

Salthouse, T.A. (1986). Perceptual, cognitive and motoric aspects of transcription typing. *Psychological Bulletin*, Vol. 99, p. 303-319.

Sandberg, J. (1994). *Human competence at work: an interpretive approach*. Göteburg: Bas.

Sandberg, J. (2000). Competence: the basis for a smart workforce. In Gerber, R.; Lankshear, C. (eds). *Training for a smart workforce*. London: Routledge, 47-72.

SCANS (1992). *Secretary's commission for achieving necessary skills*. Washington DC: Department of Labor.

Scarborough, H. (1998). Path(ological) dependency? Core competencies from an organisational perspective. *British Journal of Management*, Vol. 9, p. 219-232.

Schmid, K. (2004). *Country report: Austria*. Achieving the Lisbon Goal: the contribution of vocational education and training systems. London: Lisbon-to-Copenhagen-to-Maastricht Consortium [coordinated by QCA].

Schmidt, R.A. (1975). A schema theory of discrete motor skill learning. *Psychological Review*, Vol. 82, p. 225-260.

Schmidt, R.A. (1988). *Motor control and learning: a behavioural emphasis*. 2nd ed. Champaign, IL: Human Kinetics.

Scottish Credit and Qualifications Framework (2002). *National plan for implementation of the framework*. Edinburgh: SCQF.

Scottish Credit and Qualifications Framework (2003). *An introduction to the Scottish credit and qualification framework*. 2nd ed., Edinburgh: SCQF.

Scottish Credit and Qualifications Framework (2004). *Recognition of prior informal learning (RPL) project summary*. Edinburgh: SCQF.

Scottish Executive Health Department (2004). *Framework for developing nursing roles – consultation*. Edinburgh: SEHD.

Sellin, B. (2003). *The implications of the skills-based approach for training design: a paradigmatic shift in workrelated training and in organisational knowledge development*. Thessaloniki: Cedefop. Available from Internet: http://www2.trainingvillage.gr/download/journal/bull-28/28_en_sellin.pdf [cited 3.10.2005].

Senge, P.M. (1990). *The fifth discipline: the art and practice of the learning organisation*. New York: Doubleday.

SFIA (2004). *Introducing SFIA*. London: Skills framework for the information age. Available from Internet: http://www.sfia.org.uk [cited 3.10.2005].

Shröder, H.M. (1989). *Managerial competence: the key to excellence*. Iowa: Kendall-Hunt.

Siirala, E. (2001). The EU memorandum on lifelong learning in a nutshell. *Lifelong Learning in Europe*, Vol. 6, No 1, p. 5-6.

Singley, M.K.; Anderson, J.R. (1989). *The transfer of cognitive skill*. Cambridge, MA: Harvard University Press.

Sjöstrand, S.E. (1979). Stagnation, kris och kompetens. In Hedberg, B.; Sjöstrand, S.E. (eds). *Från företagskriser till industripolitik*, Malmö: Liber, p. 71-89.

Skills for Health (2003). *Draft competence framework for emergency services*. Edinburgh: Skills for Health.

Smith, B. (1993). Building managers from the inside out: competency based action learning. *Journal of Management Development*, Vol. 12, No 1, p. 43-48.

Smithers, A. (1993). *All our futures: Britain's education revolution*. London: Channel Four.

Smithers, A. (1997). *The New Zealand qualifications framework*. Auckland: The Education Forum.

Snoddy, G.S. (1926). Learning and stability: a psychophysiological analysis of a case of motor learning with clinical applications. *Journal of Applied Psychology*, Vol. 10, p. 1-36.

Snow, C.C.; Hrebiniak, G.L. (1980). Strategy, distinctive competence and organisational performance. *Administrative Science Quarterly*, Vol. 25, p. 317-336.

Snyder, A.; Ebeling, H.W. (1992). Targeting a company's real core competencies. *Journal of Business Strategy*, Vol. 13, No 6, p. 26-32.

Sophian, S. (1997). Beyond competence: the significance of performance for conceptual development. *Cognitive Development*, Vol. 12, p. 281-303.

Spencer, L.M. (1995). *Reengineering human resources*. New York: Wiley.

Spencer, L.M.; McClelland, D.C.; Kelner, S. (1997). *Competency assessment methods: history and state of the art*. Boston: Hay/McBer.

Spencer, L.; Spencer, S. (1993). *Competence at work: a model for superior performance*. New York: Wiley.

Stalk, G.; Evans, P.; Schulman, L.E. (1992). Competing on capabilities. *Harvard Business Review*, March-April, p. 57-69.

Stanton, G.; Richardson, W. (eds) (1997). *Qualifications for the future: a study of tripartite and other divisions in post-16 education and training*. London: Further Education Development Agency.

Stasz, C. (1997). Do employers need the skills they want? Evidence from technical work. *Journal of Education and Work*, Vol. 10, No. 3, p. 205-233.

Stäudel, T. (1987). *Problemlösen, Emotionen und Kompetenz*. Regensburg: Roederer Verlag.

Sternberg, R.J. (1977). *Intelligence, information processing and analogical reasoning: the componential analysis of human abilities*. Hillsdale, NJ: Lawrence Erlbaum.

Sternberg, R.J.; Kaufman, J.C. (1998). Human abilities. *Annual Review of Psychology*, Vol. 49, p. 479-502.

Sternberg, R.J.; Kolligian, J. (1990). *Competence considered*. New Haven: Yale University Press.

Sternberg, R.J.; Wagner, R.K. (1986). *Practical intelligence: nature and origins of competence in the everyday world*. Cambridge: Cambridge University Press.

Stewart, J.; Hamlin, B. (1992a). Competency-based qualifications: the case against change. *Journal of European Industrial Training*, Vol. 16, No 7, p. 21-32.

Stewart, J.; Hamlin, B. (1992b). Competency-based qualifications: the case for established methodologies. *Journal of European Industrial Training*, Vol. 16, No 10, p. 9-16.

Stewart, J.; Hamlin, B. (1993). Competency-based qualifications: a way forward. *Journal of European Industrial Training*, Vol. 17, No 6, p. 3-9.

Stewart, J.; Hamlin, B. (1994). Competence-based qualifications: a reply to Bob Mansfield. *Journal of European Industrial Training*, Vol. 18, No 1, p. 27-30.

Stoof, A. et al. (2002). The boundary approach of competence: a constructivist aid for understanding and using the concept of competence. *Human Resource Development Review*, Vol. 1, No 3, p. 345-365.

Straka, G.A. (2002). Valuing learning outcomes acquired in non-formal settings. In Nijhof, W.J.; Heikkinen, A.; Nieuwenhuis, L.F.M. (eds). *Shaping flexibility in vocational education and training: institutional, curricular and professional conditions*. Dordrecht: Kluwer Academic Press, p. 149-165.

Straka, G.A. (2005). Measurement and evaluation of competence. In Descy, P.; Tessaring, M. (eds). The foundations of evaluation and impact research: third report on vocational training research in Europe: background report. Luxembourg: Office for Official Publications of the European Communities, p. 263-311. Available from Internet: http://www.trainingvillage.gr/etv/ Upload/Projects_Networks/ResearchLab/ ResearchReport/BgR1_Straka. pdf [cited 3.10.2005].

Strathdee, R. (2003) The qualifications framework in New Zealand: reproducing existing inequalities or disrupting the positional conflict for credentials. *Journal of Education and Work*, Vol. 16, No 2, p. 147-164.

Strebler, M.T.; Bevan, S. (1996). *Competence-based management training*. Brighton: Institute of Employment Studies.

Stringfellow, M. (1994). Assessing for competence at Safeway stores. In Mumford, A. (ed.). *Gower Handbook of Management Development*. Aldershot: Gower, p. 293-300.

Stuart, R.; Lindsay, P. (1997). Beyond the frame of management competenc(i)es: towards a contextually embedded framework of managerial competence in organisations. *Journal of European Industrial Training*, Vol. 21, No 1, p. 26-33.

Sunoo, B.P. (1999). Creating worker competency roadmaps. *Workforce*, Vol. 78, No 3, p. 72-75.

Swift, E.J. (1904). The acquisition of skill in typewriting: a contribution to the psychology of learning. *Psychological Bulletin*, Vol. 1, p. 295-305.

Swift, E.J. (1910). Learning to telegraph. *Psychological Bulletin*, Vol. 7, p. 149-153.

Tate, W. (1995a). *Developing corporate competence: a high-performance agenda for managing organisations*. London: Gower.

Tate, W. (1995b). *Developing managerial competence: a critical guide to methods and materials*. London: Gower.

Taylor, F.W. (1911). *The principles of scientific management*. New York: Harper.

Teece, D.J.; Pisano, G.; Schuen, A. (1991). *Dynamic capabilities and strategic management*. Working paper, Center for Research in Management, University of California, Berkeley.

Thompson, J.E.; Stuart, R.; Lindsay, P.R. (1996). The competence of top teams members: a framework for successful performance. *Journal of Managerial Psychology*, Vol. 11, No 3, p. 48-66.

Thorpe, R.; Holman, D. (1997). *A critical analysis of the Management charter initiative*. Department of Management, Manchester Metropolitan University [mimeo].

Thurbin, P. (1995). *Leveraging knowledge: the 17 day program for a learning organisation*. London: Pitman.

Tobias, R. (1999). Lifelong learning under a comprehensive national qualifications framework: rhetoric and reality. *International Journal of Lifelong Education*, Vol. 18, No 2, p. 110-118.

Tobin, D.R. (1993). *Re-educating the corporation: foundations for the learning organisation*. Essex Junction, VT: Omneo.

Toussaint, R.; Xypas, C. (eds) (2004). *La notion de compétence en éducation et en formation: Fonctions et enjeux*. Paris: Editions L'Harmattan.

Tovey, L. (1993). A strategic approach to competency assessment. *Executive Development*, Vol. 7, No 10.

Training Agency (1988). *The definition of competences and performance criteria*. Guidance Note 3 in Development of Assessable Standards for National Certification Series, Sheffield: Employment Department.

Training Agency (1989). *Development of assessable standards for national certification*. Sheffield: Employment Department.

Tremblay, M.; Sire, B. (1999). Rémuner les compétences plutôt l'activité? *Revue Française de Gestion*. numéro spécial, Le retour au travail, No 126, November-December, p. 129-139.

Trépo, G.; Ferrary, M. (1997). Les enjeux méthodologiques de la gestion par les compétences. *Direction et Gestion des Entreprises*, No 164-165, March-June, p. 7-14.

Trépo, G.; Ferrary, M. (1998). La gestion des compétences: un outil stratégique. *Sciences Humaines*, Vol. 81, March, p. 34-37.

TWG (2003). *Credit transfer in VET: first report of the technical working group on credit transfer in VET*. Available from Internet: http://europa.eu.int/comm/education/ policies/2010/doc/twg_on_credit_transfer_progress_en.pdf [cited 3.10.2005].

TWG (2004). *Interim report of the technical working group*. 23 November.

United Kingdom Central Council for Nursing, Midwifery and Health Visiting (1999). *A higher level of practice: pilot standard*. London: UKCC. Available from Internet: http://www.hop.man.ac.uk/Academic/nursingmidwifery1/Learning/LatestNews/UKCCHigherlevelofpracticepilotQA.doc [cited 3.10.2005].

Unwin, L. et al. (2004). *What determines the impact of vocational qualifications? A literature review*. London: Department for Education and Skills. (Research Report, 522).

UVAC (2000). *The utilisation of NVQs in higher education in England and Wales.* London: Universities Vocational Awarding Council.

Vallas, S. (1990). The concept of skills: a critical review. *Work and Occupations,* Vol. 17, No 4, p. 379-398.

van der Klink, M.; Boon, J. (2002). The investigation of competencies within professional domains. *Human Resource Development International,* Vol. 5, No 4, p. 411-424.

Velde, C.R. (1997). Reporting the new competence needs of clerical-administrative workers: an employer perspective. *Vocational Aspect of Education,* Vol. 49, p. 21-44.

Velde, C.R. (1999). An alternative conception of competence: implications for vocational education. *Journal of Vocational Education and Training,* Vol. 51, No 3, p. 437-447.

Velde, C.R.; Hopkins, C. (1995). Reporting trainee competence: what, and how much do employers want to know? *Vocational Aspect of Education,* Vol. 46, p. 5-11.

Vind, A.; Delamare Le Deist, F.; Heidemann, W.; Winterton, J. (2004). *European Trade Union policies on lifelong learning.* Copenhagen: Landsorganisationen i Danmark.

Waddington, S. (2000). A memorandum on lifelong learning. *Adults Learning,* Vol. 12, No 4, p. 15-17.

Wagner, R.K.; Sternberg, R.J. (1986). Tacit knowledge and intelligence in the everyday world. In Sternberg, R.J.; Wagner, R.K. (eds). *Practical intelligence: nature and origins of competence in the everyday world.* Cambridge: Cambridge University Press, p. 51-83.

Weick, K.E. (1991). The nontraditional quality of organisational learning. *Organisational Science,* Vol. 2, No 1, p. 116-124.

Weinert, F.E. (1999). *Concepts of competence.* Munich: Max Planck Institute for Psychological Research. Published as a contribution to the OECD project Definition and selection of competencies: theoretical and conceptual foundations (DeSeCo). Neuchâtel: DeSeCo.

Weinert, F.E. (2001). Vergleichende Leistungsmessung in Schulen: eine umstrittene Selbstverständlichkeit. In Weinert, F.E. (ed.). *Leistungsmessungen in Schulen.* Weinheim: Beltz Verlag, p. 17-31.

Welford, A.T. (1968). *Fundamentals of skill.* London: Methuen.

Welford, A.T. (1976). *Skilled performance: perceptual and motor skills.* Glenview, IL: Scott, Foresman.

White, R.H. (1959). Motivation reconsidered: the concept of competence. *Psychological Review,* Vol. 66, p. 279-333.

Whitely, R. (1989). On the nature of managerial tasks and skills: their distinguishing characteristics and organisation. *Journal of Management Studies,* Vol. 26, No 3, p. 209-224.

Wilson, L.S.; Boudreaux, M.A.; Edwards, M. (2000). High performance leadership at the individual level. *Advances in developing human resources*, Vol. 6, p. 73-103.

Winterton, J. (2000). The role of work organisation in developing competence at work: a study of four workplaces in the UK. Cedefop European Seminar *Key qualifications: from theory to practice*, Sintra, 5-6 June.

Winterton, J. (2003). *Social dialogue and vocational training in the EU: analysis of a Cedefop survey*. Thessaloniki: Cedefop.

Winterton, J. (2004). Improving the effectiveness of social partner involvement in VET research. Cedefop Agora *Vocational education and training in Europe: to what end?* Thessaloniki, 16-17 February. Thessaloniki: Cedefop.

Winterton, J. et al. (2000). *Future skill needs of managers*. Sheffield: Department for Education and Employment. (Research Report, 182).

Winterton, J.; Winterton, R. (1994). *Collective bargaining and consultation over continuing vocational training*. RM.7, Sheffield: Employment Department.

Winterton, J.; Winterton, R. (1996). *The business benefits of competence-based management development*. London: HMSO. (Department for Education and Employment Research Studies, 16)

Winterton, J.; Winterton, R. (1997). Workplace training and enskilling. In Walters, S. (ed.). *Globalization, adult education and training: impacts and issues*. London: Zed Books, p. 154-64.

Winterton, J.; Winterton, R. (1998). *Validation and recognition of competences and qualifications in the UK: final UK report of Leonardo da Vinci project VALID*. Employment Research Institute, Napier University.

Winterton, J.; Winterton, R. (1999). *Developing managerial competence*. London: Routledge.

Winterton, J.; Winterton, R. (2002a). Implementing management standards in the UK. *Academy of Human Resource Development Annual Conference: proceedings* Vol. 2, p. 974-981.

Winterton, J.; Winterton, R. (2002b). Forecasting skill needs in the UK clothing industry. *Journal of Fashion Marketing and Management*, Vol. 6, No 4, p. 352-362.

Wolf, A. (1995). *Competence-based assessment*. Buckingham: Open University Press.

Wolf, A. (1998). Competence-based assessment: does it shift the demarcation line? In Nijhof, W.J.; Streumer, J.N. (eds). *Key qualifications in work and education*. Dordrecht: Kluwer Academic Press, p. 207-220.

Wood, R.; Power, C. (1987). Aspects of the competence-performance distinction: educational, psychological and measurement issues. *Journal of Curriculum Studies*, Vol. 19, No 5, p. 409-424.

Woodruffe, C. (1990). *Assessment centres: identifying and developing competence*. London: Institute of Personnel Management.

Woodruffe, C. (1991). Competent by any other name. *Personnel Management*, September, p. 30-33.

Young. M. (2003). National qualifications as a global phenomenon: a comparative perspective. *Journal of Education and Work*, Vol. 16, No 3, p. 223-237.

Zarifian, P. (1999a). *Objectif Compétence: pour une nouvelle logique*. Paris: Liaisons.

Zarifian, P. (1999b). Productivité, logique de service et mutations du travail. *Revue Française de Gestion*, numéro spécial, Le retour au travail, No 126, November-December, p. 106-116.

Zarifian, P. (2000). Sur la question de la compétence. *Gérer et comprendre*, December, p. 25-28.

Zenke, S.; Zenke, R. (1999). Putting competencies to work. *Training*, Vol. 36, No 1, p. 70-76.

Respondents providing information

Austria: Leonardo da Vinci project DISCO
Claudia Plaimauer
3s (superior skills solutions), Vienna
E-mail: plaimauer@3s.co.at

Czech Republic
Hana Čiiháková
National Institute of Technical and Vocational Education, Prague
E-mail: cihakova@nuov.cz

Finland
Ulpukka Isopahkala
University of Helsinki
E-mail: isopahka@mappi.helsinki.fi

Sirkka-Liisa Kärki
National Board of Education, Helsinki
E-mail: sirkka-liisa.karki@oph.fi

France
Henriette Perker
Centre pour le Développement de l'Information sur la Formation Permanente, Paris
E-mail: h.perker@centre.inffo.fr

Hugues Bertrand,
CEREQ, Marseille
E-mail: bertrand@cereq.fr

Annie Bouder
CEREQ, Marseille
E-mail: bouder@cereq.fr

Sylvie-Anne Mériot
CEREQ, Marseille
E-mail: meriot@cereq.fr

Germany
Dr. Georg Hanf
BIBB - Bundesinstitut für Berufsbildung
E-mail: Hanf@bibb.de

Prof Dr Gerald A. Straka
Universität Bremen/ITB
E-mail: straka@uni-bremen.de

Hungary
Viktória Szilasi
National Centre for Vocational Training, Budapest
E-mail: szilasi.viktoria@om.hu

Ireland
Edwin Mernagh
National Qualifications Authority, Dublin
E-mail: emernagh@nqai.ie

Jean Wrigley
FÁS-Training and Employment Authority, Dublin
E-mail: jean.wrigley@fas.ie

Italy
Enrica Flamini
Ministry of Education, Rome
E-mail: enrica.flamini@istruzione.it

Netherlands
Mirjam de Jong
VAPRO-OVP (HR Developers in the Process Industry), Amsterdam
E-mail: M.d.Jong@vapro-ovp.com

Martine Broere
Innovam (Knowledge Centre in the Automotive Sector), Amsterdam
E-mail: m.broere@Innovam.nl

Christof Wielemaker
COLO (Association of national centres of expertise on VET/labour market),
Amsterdam
E-mail: c.wielemaker@colo.nl

Portugal
Ana Claudia Valente
Institute for Quality in Training (formerly INOFOR), Lisbon
E-mail: ana.valente@inofor.gov.pt

Dr Antonio M Palma
Ministry of Education, Lisbon
E-mail: antonio.palma@des.min-edu.pt

Slovakia
Andrea Hagovská
Slovak Management and Training Centre, Bratislava
E-mail: performr@stonline.sk

Spain
Jose Luis Garcia
Ministry of Education, Madrid
E-mail: joseluis.garcia@educ.mec.es

The United Kingdom – England and Wales
Dr Laurence Solkin
Centre for Professional Development and Innovation, City University, London
E-mail: l.solkin@city.ac.uk

Professor Jim Stewart
Nottingham Business School
E-mail: jim.stewart@ntu.ac.uk

Professor Lorna Unwin
Centre for Labour Market Studies, University of Leicester
E-mail: l.unwin@le.ac.uk

The United Kingdom – Scotland
Professor Jim McGoldrick
Chairman, Fife National Health Service Board, Dundee
E-mail: james.mcgoldrick@nhs.net

Annex 2 General descriptors for European reference levels

European reference level	Draft general descriptors for European reference levels
1	Learning normally acquired during compulsory education and considered as contributing to a general knowledge and development of basic skills. Learning is not usually contextualised in work situations.
2	Completion of compulsory education which includes an induction to work. Basic knowledge of work can be acquired at an educational establishment, in an out-of-school training programme or in an enterprise. Generally it is not occupation specific. The range of knowledge, skills and competence involved is limited. Qualification at this level indicates a person can perform basic tasks and exercise repetitive skills in a controlled environment. All action appears to be governed by rules defining allowable routines and strategies.
3	Completion of a basic vocational training qualification introducing the idea of job competence. It is normally considered part of upper secondary education. This qualification shows a person has basic skills suitable for many job functions and the capacity to carry out tasks under direction. Most action of people at this level of qualification is deliberate repetitive application of knowledge and skills.
4	Qualification at this level normally includes upper secondary education and a work-based training programme in an alternance or apprenticeship scheme and involves developing knowledge linked to a specific occupational sector. People qualified at this level are able to work independently on tasks and have the capacity to apply specialist knowledge, skills and competences. They will have extensive experience and practice in both common and exceptional situations and be able to solve problems independently using this experience.
5	Completion of a main vocational training qualification such as apprenticeship or higher education training. This form of qualification involves significant theoretical knowledge and involves mainly technical work that can be performed independently and entail supervisory and coordination duties. Qualification at this level indicates a person can deal with complex situations and their performance can be a benchmark for others. They will have considerable experience and practice across a wide range of work situations. This qualification level often bridges secondary and tertiary education and training.

European reference level	Draft general descriptors for European reference levels
6	Qualification at this level covers a high level of theoretical and practical knowledge, skill and competence, entailing a mastery of the scientific basis of an occupation. Qualification at this level means a person can deal comfortably with complex situations is generally autonomous and can assume design, management and administrative responsibilities. They are equivalent to undergraduate honours degrees. Study for these qualifications outside work takes place mostly in higher education institutions.
7	These qualifications recognise specialist theoretical and practical learning that is required for work as (senior) professionals and managers. People qualified at this level will have a wide breadth and depth of knowledge and be able to demonstrate high levels of specialist competence in an area. They will operate independently and supervise and train others where they can be inspiring. These qualifications are equivalent to masters' degrees. Study for these qualifications outside work takes place in specialist higher education institutions.
8	These qualifications recognise people as leading experts in a highly specialised field dealing with complex situations and having the capacity for long-range strategic and scientific thinking and action. Such experts develop new and creative approaches that extend or redefine existing knowledge or professional practice and often teach others to be experts and masters. The qualifications are equivalent to doctoral qualifications. Study for these qualifications outside work takes place mostly in specialist higher education institutions.

Source: DG Education and Culture note *Developing common reference levels to underpin a European qualifications framework*, 24.9.2004.

Annex 3 Use of competence frameworks in the UK health sector

Throughout the United Kingdom, frameworks for KSCs have been extensively used in the health sector for over a decade. As in other sectors, strategic workforce development in health is overseen by a sector skills council: Skills for health was established in April 2002 with support from the four UK health departments, the independent and voluntary health sectors and staff organisations. Occupational standards, applicable across the United Kingdom, are developed by skills for health in cooperation with other parties and in accordance with the technical criteria established by QCA (SQA in Scotland).

The National health service (NHS) knowledge and skills framework (KSF), a development tool that is also used to support decisions about pay progression, comprises several dimensions: six have been defined as core to the NHS and will occur in every occupation, while a further 16 specific dimensions relate to some jobs and not others. Individuals need to apply the knowledge and skills in several dimensions to achieve the expectations of their job. Most jobs will be made up of the core dimensions and between three and six specific dimensions, although a few jobs might involve more than this.

The core dimensions in the NHS KSF are:
(1) communication,
(2) personal and people development,
(3) health, safety and security,
(4) service development,
(5) quality,
(6) equality, diversity and rights.

The specific dimensions in the NHS KSF are:
(7) assessing health and wellbeing needs,
(8) addressing individuals' health and wellbeing needs,
(9) improving health and wellbeing,
(10) protecting health and wellbeing,
(11) logistics,
(12) data processing and management,
(13) producing and communicating information and knowledge,
(14) facilities maintenance and management,
(15) designing and producing equipment, devices and visual records,

(16) biomedical investigation and reporting,
(17) measuring, monitoring and treating physiological conditions through applying specific technologies,
(18) partnership,
(19) leadership,
(20) managing people,
(21) managing physical and financial resources,
(22) research and development.

Each dimension of the NHS KSF is further elaborated by a series of level descriptors, which show successively more advanced knowledge and skill and/or the increasing complexity of applying knowledge and skills to the demands of work. Each level builds on the preceding level(s). The number of level descriptors varies from one dimension to another (although this is being kept under review in case development work reveals there to be a set number across all of the dimensions). Attached to each level descriptor are indicators, which describe the level at which knowledge and skills need to be applied and are designed to enable more consistent and reliable application of the dimensions and descriptors across the NHS.

The nursing and midwifery council (NMC) sets several requirements for practice covering general, mental health, children's, learning disabilities nursing and midwifery and as the statutory and regulatory body for nursing and midwifery, determines the standards of practice to be achieved at the point of registration, at diploma level. The standards of proficiency for pre-registration nursing education (NMC, 2004) outline knowledge and skills in relation to contextual learning. The professional code of conduct (NMC, 2002a) underpins the behavioural components. The standards of proficiency define the overarching principles of being able to practice as a nurse; the context in which they are achieved defines the scope of professional practice. All of the standards reflect the requirements of the EC nursing directives.

The standards of proficiency for pre-registration nursing education were developed in support of the Nursing and Midwifery Council (education, registration and registration appeals) rules 2004. These rules and standards of proficiency replace all previous requirements for pre-registration nursing programmes issued by the NMC or previously the United Kingdom Central Council for Nursing, Midwifery and Health Visiting (UKCC) and the four National Boards for England, Northern Ireland, Scotland and Wales. Their status is mandatory, in accordance with statutory legislation. There are eight standards related to pre-registration nursing education, which specify structural requirements in relation to content, length of programmes, context and nature of programmes, linking basic knowledge (theory and practice) and assessment strategies, including Accreditation of Prior (Experiential) Learning (APEL) under Standard 3:

> The Council will allow accreditation of prior learning against any part of the programme where the applicant is able to demonstrate relevant prior learning to the satisfaction of the approved educational institution and in accordance with the Council's requirements and guidance on APEL. (NMC, 2002a, p. 10).

Following registration, several competence frameworks apply depending upon the level and specialism pursued. The second level of the nursing part of the register is open only for those nurses previously qualified in the United Kingdom who continue to practice as second level nurses and to second level nurses from the European economic area (EEA) who wish to exercise their right to freedom of movement. The standards of proficiency for second level nursing are known as threshold standards; they enable second level nurses to undertake care under the direction of a first level registered nurse, but do not imply an immutable limit on the practice of second level registered nurses.

The UKCC (forerunner of the NMC) established a post-registration education and practice project, which in 1994 identified two levels of practice beyond the point of registration - advanced and specialist. Explicit standards in the form of learning outcomes were set for specialist practice and a conceptual descriptor of advanced practice was offered. Standards for this higher level of practice are threshold and generic (in the sense of applicable across all health care settings) and are concerned with level of practice, not specialty or role. The *higher level of practice project report* (NMC, 2002b) reviews and evaluates the work on higher level of practice (HLP) over the past decade. In 1999, HLP pilot standards were defined detailing seven competencies:

- providing effective health care,
- improving quality and health outcomes,
- evaluation and research,
- leading and developing practice,
- innovation and changing practice,
- developing self and others,
- working across professional and organisational boundaries.

Each competence is elaborated in terms of activities, so, for example in the case of 'developing self and others', the HLP pilot standards prescribe that: practitioners working at a higher level:

- are proactive in developing and improving their own competence in structured ways, including accessing inter-professional clinical supervision;
- develop and use appropriate strategies and opportunities to share

knowledge with, and influence the practice of patients, clients, carers and other practitioners of differing status, while remaining self-aware and understanding the limits of their own competence;

- work collaboratively with others to plan and deliver interventions to meet the learning and development needs of their own and other professions;
- lobby for sufficient resources to improve the learning and practice of their own and other professions in the interests of patients and clients (UKCC, 1999, p. 4).

A glossary of terms in the HLP pilot standards notes that different models of competence have different theoretical roots: 'The model used for the standard of a higher level of practice focuses on the outcomes which any individual working at a higher level has to achieve in their practice. This is in contrast to other models of competence which describe, for example, the personal characteristics of individuals, the outcomes which individuals need to achieve at the end of a specific learning programme, or the tasks which an individual needs to undertake'. Outcomes are defined as 'the results of practice rather than the activities or tasks which lead to the result. Outcomes may be tangible or intangible. Tangible outcomes are the result of physical activity, such as a product which can be physically examined. An intangible outcome is the result of a cognitive or interactive process, such as a decision' (UKCC, 1999, p. 6).

The Annex to a recent paper by NHS education for Scotland proposed skill components for staff involved in out-of-hours roles, including 14 occupations as different as general medical practitioners, nurse practitioners, pharmacists, social workers and transport workers. Each of the occupations covered has been mapped against existing competency frameworks with the aim of identifying competencies that already exist across the sector rather than defining new ones for a specific role:

The National Evaluation Systems, Emergency nurse practitioners, skills for health emergency care framework and the NHS24 competencies provide a good match against the proposed components and have been used to give a broad framework within which key criteria statements can be developed. These also provide the framework upon which assessment of competence, by knowledge, skills and attitude can be measured. Drilling down within both these frameworks to, for example, the performance indicator statements from the NHS24 framework, gives further detail that can be used to support assessment. Further specific competency frameworks related to, for example diabetes, have also been mapped. Additional work on practice nurse competencies may well offer additional supporting material. As the Remote and Rural Areas Resource Initiative (RARARI) competencies are further developed, these may reflect the specific healthcare needs presented within the rural context. Other professional competencies from among the ambulance service, Allied Health Professions and general practitioners themselves will help to inform this process.

There is continuing work about the appropriate competence expected of practitioners, and a general sense that this may vary in different clinical contexts. Certainly implementing this framework will, at least in the short term, create a service model within which practitioners are functioning across a broad continuum of competence/expertise. Given the dynamic nature of this implementation process, we may not yet be in a position to identify the optimum level at which each practitioner in the skill mix should be operating. However, this initial mapping does support this discussion. Educational providers in higher education institutions, the independent sector and within NHS Boards can use these competencies to work together with professional colleagues to frame their programmes of study for practitioner development. Existing programmes of study in this area also have competency statements linked to educational and practice outcomes and these outcomes can be mapped against this initial framework. The consultation process and subsequent discussions with service and education partners have shown a high congruence between the framework and perceived need.

There remain some components for which national competency frameworks have not been developed. Discussions with clinicians and educators have suggested that management protocols and best practice guidance do exist for many of these. This additional information will be mapped against these components. Again, the goal is that of achieving a broad multi-professional consensus on best practice (NHS education for Scotland, 2004, p. 23-24).

Annex 4 # Competence framework for process operators (the Netherlands)

Individual competence details – 1

Operating machinery, performing plant operation procedures	Knowledge		Skill	Assessed performance
	Basic	Further		
1. Able to start or stop the process, plant and machinery according to procedure in normal operation	x		x	x
2. Able to start or stop the process, plant and machinery according to procedure in emergency situations	x	x	x	x
3. Able to monitor process, plant and machinery requirements and conditions within the task	x	x	x	x
4. Able to respond to safety, economic and environmental requirements within the task	x		x	x
5. Able to make appropriate changes based on the state of the plant at that time	x	x	x	x
6. Able to exchange information about the task with team members and others	x			
7. Able to coach team members and others in the key tasks in this job		x	x	x
8. Able to correctly update the documentation and logs according to procedure	x		x	x
9. Able to correctly communicate with other plant areas affected by the job	x		x	

Individual competence details – 2

Operating machinery, performing plant operation procedures	Knowledge		Skill	Assessed performance
	Basic	Further		
1. Able to describe the basic operations and basic functions of the software and can assign them to the process controlled system and its main components	x		x	x
2. Able to describe and explain processes and their visualisation on the screen		x	x	x
3. Able to prepare the system to start an operating process manually and by means of operating software	x		x	x
4. Able to start a process controlled system (basic operations, parts of recipes, recipes) manually and via software and screen	x		x	x
5. Able to operate and control processes manually and via software and screen	x		x	x
6. Able to analyse alarm messages and take the right actions (stop the process correct the process or other actions)	x		x	x
7. Able to assign the different steps of a running process to the process controlled system and its main components		x	x	x
8. Able to document faultlessly the different steps of a whole process according to the Standard Operating Procedures (SOP)		x	x	x
9. Able to complete a running process and clean the process controlled system via software and screen	x		x	x
10. Able to start up, operate and shut down production plants with the help of regular control technology components or process control technology	x		x	x
11. Able to perform in-process checks	x		x	x
12. Has a fundamental understanding of the basic production process	x		x	
13. Has a fundamental understanding of process control and instrumentation technologies	x		x	
14. Able to distinguish between critical an uncritical measurement data		x	x	x

	Basic		Skill	Performance
15. Knowing the cause-effect relationships of the process and the control and process technology and is able to interpret these		X	X	X
16. Able to read and interpret piping and instrumentation flowcharts	X		X	
17. Able to operate IT-equipment (information and telecommunication) like PC, touch screen, joystick, printer	X		X	

Individual competence details – 3

Analysis of the process, fault finding and problem solving	Knowledge		Skill	Assessed performance
	Basic	Further		
1. Able to monitor the process and recognise faults and problems during the process	X		X	X
2. Able to check the function and identify faults		X	X	X
3. Able to quickly respond to faults which can cause safety and/or environmental problems		X	X	X
4. Able to make changes and adjustments of the production depending on faults detected		X	X	X
5. Able to judge problems and prioritise decisions		X	X	X
6. Able to report problems and faults according to procedures within the company	X		X	X
7. Able to communicate correctly with manufacturing companies, maintenance companies, etc. for the production equipment	X		X	X

Individual competence details – 4

Responding to process hazardous problems, performing operative emergency procedures	Knowledge		Skill	Assessed performance
	Basic	Further		
1. Able to discern between a process upset and a process emergency situation	X		X	X
2. Able to assess rudimentally the potential hazard of the process upset to personnel, plant and environment	X		X	X

		Basic	Further	Skill	Assessed performance
3.	Able to quickly identify a basic approach for a solution to react to a hazardous problem		x	x	x
4.	Able to alarm, to start emergency procedures, to call authoritative/ supervisory staff	x		x	x
5.	Able to use operating and emergency procedures as a guide to take the correct actions until authoritative assistance arrives	x		x	x
6.	Able to establish an initial response that will act to neutralise or minimise the effect of a developing emergency situation		x	x	x
7.	Able to monitor and direct all operations in hazardous situations concerning the safety of the plant, personnel and environment until authoritative assistance arrives	x		x	x
8.	Able to report on the process upset clearly and accurately	x		x	x
9.	Able to manage his operating team during the emergency procedure in a calm and efficient manner		x	x	x
10.	Able to maintain safety equipment and materials required for emergency response, which belong to the plant	x		x	x
11.	Able to maintain a state of readiness through self and team development activities	x		x	x

Individual competence details – 5

		Knowledge		Skill	Assessed performance
Executing logistic jobs		**Basic**	**Further**		
1.	Able to realise the plan of production schedules	x		x	x
2.	Able to liaise with suppliers to ensure supplier has adequate back up stock levels	x		x	x
3.	Able to understand/compare the required specification for supplies and products	x		x	x
4.	Able to maintain accurate records and documentation	x		x	x

		Basic	Further	Skill	Assessed performance
5.	Able to carry out/ensure all quality checks prior to supplies being used or products being dispatched		x	x	x
6.	Able to respond to changes in the planned production schedule		x	x	x
7.	Able to arrange and manage deliveries		x	x	x
8.	Able to arrange and manage dispatches		x	x	x
9.	Able to manage hazards including handling and safe disposal according to environmental rules and procedures	x			

Individual competence details – 6

Maintaining quality control		Knowledge		Skill	Assessed performance
		Basic	Further		
1.	Able to take samples	x		x	x
2.	Able to take quality measurements according to procedure		x	x	x
3.	Able to decide, on the basis of the measurements, whether the product meets the required specifications and/or standards		x	x	x
4.	Able to report in the correct way on the results of the quality measurements	x		x	x
5.	Able to intervene in the event of deviation from the specifications, by adjusting or stopping production in accordance with procedures		x	x	x
6.	Act promptly to consult the supervisor in the case of complex situations	x	x	x	x
7.	Able to aim, together with colleagues, for quality improvement and can deal pro-actively with regard to quality improvement using relevant models and methods of process development and process improvement	x	x	x	x
8.	Able to work in accordance with regulations (quality, working conditions, safety and environmental-regulations)	x	x	x	x

Individual competence details – 7

Monitoring maintenance work and safety working conditions	Knowledge		Skill	Assessed performance
	Basic	Further		
1. Able to shut down, isolate and prepare process units or production equipment for maintenance	x	x	x	x
2. Able to use operating procedures, administrative checks, emergency response and other management approaches to prevent incidents or to minimise the effect of an incident by hot-work procedures and confined space entry permits	x	x	x	x
3. Able to communicate correctly with maintenance staff to realise planned work order procedures and check and test the final results of work done		x	x	x
4. Able to monitor own or contractor maintenance work and identify unsafe and improper working procedures and conditions		x	x	x
5. Able to perform and monitor minor repair and maintenance work according to audited procedures on mechanical, electrical and instrument field		x	x	x
6. Able to assist and cooperate with maintenance personnel during refurbishing, de-bottlenecking and turnaround activities	x	x	x	x
7. Able to organise and use tools, machinery, equipment, chemicals and energy for doing proper and safe maintenance work	x		x	x
8. Able to understand and monitor equipment and procedures for preventive maintenance techniques		x	x	x
9. Able to monitor the use of reliable equipment and working methods during maintenance work		x	x	x
10. Able to identify and use proper personnel safety material and equipment	x		x	x

Individual competence details – 8

Performing maintenance	Knowledge		Skill	Assessed performance
	Basic	Further		
1. Able to consult equipment manuals				x
2. Able to work in accordance with working regulations		x		x
3. Able to adjust installation for change of product (in accordance with planning and regulations)		x	x	x
4. Able to prioritise the urgency to consult colleagues or specialists about necessary maintenance				x
5. Able to use the correct tools for carrying out maintenance work	x		x	x
6. Able to check things over after work has been carried out (before the installation is used again)				x
7. Able to consult the maintenance department and to work together with them	x		x	x
8. Able to ensure that conditions (hygiene, safety) are maintained for production	x			x
9. Able to work in accordance with regulations (quality, working conditions, safety and environmental-regulations)	x			x
10. Able to use the correct personal protective equipment	x	x	x	x

Individual competence details – 9

Working according to health, safety, labour law and environmental requirements	Knowledge		Skill	Assessed performance
	Basic	Further		
1. Know the characteristics and understand the behaviour of the handled substances	x			
2. Able to associate characteristics of substances with the law and occupational health	x			
3. Know and understand the safety rules	x			
4. Know the physical interrelations concerning the emergence of fire and explosion	x			
5. Able to associate the knowledge of fire and explosion with personal behaviour	x			

	Basic	Further	Skill	Assessed performance
6. Able to associate process parameters with danger for humans, equipment and environment	x			x
7. Able to foresee the results of behaviour against the laws and rules of safety and health	x	x	x	x
8. Able to handle responsibly chemicals, energy and other substances or hazards involved		x		x
9. Able to use the correct personal protective equipment	x	x		x
10. Able to manage the process wearing personal protective clothing			x	x
11. Able to make prompt important decisions		x		x
12. Know and understand the local emergency laws		x		
13. Able to admit responsibility for own and others' health, equipment and the environment			x	x
14. Able to realise the valid laws for working time, with regard to working under pressure		x		x
15. Able to understand the interaction between safety, quality and the economy		x		

Individual competence details – 10

Working in teams	Knowledge		Skill	Assessed performance
	Basic	Further		
1. Know his own responsibilities and to know what needs to be settled with the supervisor (malfunctions, defects, safety, working conditions, etc.)	x			x
2. Able to give equal value within a team to everyone's standpoint or vision			x	x
3. Able to share relevant information and experience that is important for the working process with others in the team and able to use information received from others			x	x
4. Able to put the joint result of the team above the achievement of his own results			x	x

		Knowledge			
5.	Able to take into account the possible consequences of individual actions for others within the team	x		x	x
6.	Able to challenge team members, even if it concerns complex/sensitive issues			x	x
7.	Has enough command of the terminology of other disciplines for discussions	x	x		
8.	Able to act adequately in conflict situations			x	x
9.	Able to deal constructively with criticism from others, does not let this influence his own work			x	x
10.	Able to contribute constructively to different forms of work discussions in the team			x	x
11.	Able to make a clear transfer of work (preparing for the next shift)	x	x	x	x
12.	Able to administrate/register his work in a comprehensible way	x	x	x	x
13.	Able to work in accordance with regulations (quality, working conditions, safety and environmental-regulations)	x	x		

Individual competence details – 11

Communicating with internal suppliers, customers and services		Knowledge		Skill	Assessed performance
		Basic	Further		
1.	Able to communicate freely using the terminology, abbreviations, plant nomenclature and equipment tag numbering systems	x			
2.	Able to complete log sheets, sample results, product quality certificates, maintenance request forms, reports and any other written forms required by the day to day running of the plant	x			
3.	Able to understand the significance of forms and how the data is used within other departments	x	x		
4.	Able to gather, translate and transfer relevant data, communicating any variations and be aware of the effect any variations will have	x	x		
5.	Able to order consumable supplies through an approved procedure	x			

		Basic	Further		
6.	Able to understand the specification for supplies and the effect on the process or product of any variations they may have	X	X		
7.	Know and understand the material handling hazards associated with all materials used and stored within the working area	X	X		
8.	Able to recognise types of packing and the meaning of label symbols and abbreviations	X			
9.	Able to estimate requirements for material against suppliers stock levels to ensure production targets	X	X	X	X
10.	Able to understand the structure of plant support services and departments and be able to communicate plant needs through recognised channels and procedures	X	X	X	X
11.	Able to administer Permit systems and manage the conditions laid down for maintenance work and procedures	X	X		
12.	Able to understand the structure of line management and their levels of authority	X	X		

Individual competence details – 12

Dealing with changes and information		Knowledge		Skill	Assessed performance
		Basic	Further		
1.	Able to take initiative in following new developments			X	X
2.	Able to share expertise with colleagues			X	X
3.	Able to contribute to improvements in the production process	X	X	X	
4.	Able to contribute to product innovation	X	X	X	
5.	Able to think along the lines of cost consciousness	X	X		
6.	Able to recognise and formulate the own information needs for carrying out his tasks	X			
7.	Able to look efficiently for sources of information	X		X	

	Basic	Further	Skill	Assessed performance
8. Able to use information from various sources: handbooks, reports, intranet, Internet	x		x	
9. Able to study available documentation about the process or the installation	x		x	
10. Able to use documents (manuals, etc.) in modern languages (specialist terms in native language and in English)	x	x	x	x
11. Able to distil the necessary information from a document	x		x	
12. Able to remain informed – within own level – about developments related to the profession	x	x	x	x
13. Able to help colleagues to find necessary details	x	x	x	x

Individual competence details – 13

Coaching colleague operators	Knowledge		Skill	Assessed performance
	Basic	Further		
1. Able to use the technical terminology of chemical engineering to describe normal processes in the chemical production			x	
2. Able to describe characteristic chemical part-automated or automated production processes of his plant and explain the basic functions of the different processes			x	
3. Able to introduce and instruct apprentices and unskilled colleagues in the different steps of the used production processes taking responsible care into consideration			x	x
4. Able to discuss problems and troubles of the production process or a single step of the process with his colleagues and able to speak about trouble shooting			x	
5. Able to demonstrate simple communication rules	x		x	x
6. Able to prepare simple presentations	x		x	x
7. Able to make factual and understandable contributions to discussions			x	
8. Able to place him/herself in the position of other colleagues			x	x

Individual competence details – 14

Handling information, for example written and electronic documentation	Knowledge		Skill	Assessed performance
	Basic	Further		
1. Able to read, write, calculate and understand written and electronic documentation	X	X		X
2. Able to use intranet and Internet (e-mail, search engine, personal organiser ...) to exchange documents about the task	X	X	X	X
3. Able to handle documentation about the process responsibly and correctly			X	
4. Able to hand over correctly documentation about the process from one shift to the following shift			X	
5. Able to fill in and update correctly the necessary documentation about the process, products and safety instructions		X	X	
6. Able to exchange responsibly information about the process, about updates and about safety instructions with team members			X	

Potentially relevant Leonardo da Vinci projects

N°	Year	Sector	Theme/task	Title	Web Page
4	2001	Agriculture, hunting and related service activities	Curricula development certification and validation of qualifications (competencies)	ESA4 – European sustainable agriculture education level 4	http://leonardo. cec.eu.int/pdb/ Detail_En_2000. cfm?Numero=1129 322&Annee=2001
37	2001	Education	Curricula development certification and validation of qualifications (competencies)	INCA – A project to develop a framework, diagnostic tool and record of competence for the assessment of intercultural competence integrated with language competence and subject knowledge competence	http://leonardo. cec.eu.int/pdb/ Detail_En_2000. cfm?Numero=1129 315&Annee=2001
52	2001	Education (2) [183]	Skills assessment certification and validation of qualifications (competencies)	Self-evaluation – Transnational methods and models for self-evaluation of non-formal personal competencies	http://leonardo. cec.eu.int/pdb/ Detail_En_2000. cfm?Numero=1080 502&Annee=2001
64	2001	Education (2) [157]	Sectoral development certification and validation of qualifications (competencies)	EuroCertStaff in SME Sector – training and certification of SME staff in the crafts and services sector according to European	http://leonardo. cec.eu.int/pdb/ Detail_En_2000. cfm?Numero=1134 053&Annee=2001

N°	Year	Sector	Theme/task	Title	Web Page
72	2001	Electricity, gas, steam and hot water supply (1) [117]	Certification and validation of qualifications (competencies) Curricula development	ENERSOL EU – strengthening vocational education in the field of energy saving and sustainable energy	http://leonardo.cec.eu.int/pdb/Detail_En_2000.cfm?Numero=1123143&Annee=2001
75	2001	Financial intermedia-tion, except insurance and pension funding	Certification and validation of qualifications (competencies)	EFCB – European foundation certificate in banking	http://leonardo.cec.eu.int/pdb/Detail_En_2000.cfm?Numero=1084904&Annee=2001
87	2001	Health and social work	Curricula development certification and validation of qualifications (competencies)	EuroPsy (€) – Project to design a European diploma of psychology	http://leonardo.cec.eu.int/pdb/Detail_En_2000.cfm?Numero=1129444&Annee=2001
157	2001	Other service activities (1) [64]	Sectoral development certification and validation of qualifications (competencies)	EuroCertStaff in SME Sector – training and certification of SME staff in the crafts and services sector according to European	http://leonardo.cec.eu.int/pdb/Detail_En_2000.cfm?Numero=1134053&Annee=2001
160	2001	Other service activities (2) [104]	Certification and validation of qualifications (competencies) sectoral development	NATURAE – A Comparative Analysis of Professional and Training Needs within the Environmental Tourism Sector	http://leonardo.cec.eu.int/pdb/Detail_En_2000.cfm?Numero=1081505&Annee=2001
181	2001	Research and devel-opment	Curricula development certification and validation of qualifications (competencies)	EURO-MTEC – European marine technology education consortium	http://leonardo.cec.eu.int/pdb/Detail_En_2000.cfm?Numero=1129370&Annee=2001

N°	Year	Sector	Theme/task	Title	Web Page
183	2001	Research and development (1) [52]	Skills assessment certification and validation of qualifications (competencies)	SELF-EVALUATION – Transnational methods and models for self-evaluation of non-formal personal competencies	http://leonardo.cec.eu.int/pdb/Detail_En_2000.cfm?Numero=1080502&Annee=2001
190	2001	Retail trade, except of motor vehicles and motorcycles; repair of personal and household goods (2) [105]	Training of trainers certification and validation of qualifications (competencies)	PRACTICERT – Accreditation and certification of work-related qualifications during job placements	http://leonardo.cec.eu.int/pdb/Detail_En_2000.cfm?Numero=1084715&Annee=2001
24	2002	Collection, purification and distribution of water (2) [70] [75]	Certification and validation of qualifications (competencies) training modules	Opti-Gas – Optimising the use of natural gas	http://leonardo.cec.eu.int/pdb/Detail_En_2000.cfm?Numero=2112613&Annee=2002
25	2002	Computer and related activities (1) [198]	Certification and validation of qualifications (competencies) Curricula development	DB Tech Pro	http://leonardo.cec.eu.int/pdb/Detail_En_2000.cfm?Numero=2126706&Annee=2002
35	2002	Construction (1) [189]	Certification and validation of qualifications (competencies) Training modules Sectoral development	Recognition of qualification: model of professional qualification structure and new methods of promotion, certification and mutual recognition of managerial skills in construction industry according to the requirements of E.U.	http://leonardo.cec.eu.int/pdb/Detail_En_2000.cfm?Numero=2140029&Annee=2002

N°	Year	Sector	Theme/task	Title	Web Page
62	2002	Education (2) [122]	Certification and validation of qualifications (competencies) Skills assessment	Partnership for competency evaluation	http://leonardo. cec.eu.int/pdb/ Detail_En_2000. cfm?Numero=2115 825&Annee=2002
106	2002	Health and social work (2) [54]	Sectoral development skills assessment	EHTAN – European healthcare training and accreditation network	http://leonardo. cec.eu.int/pdb/ Detail_En_2000. cfm?Numero=2129 583&Annee=2002
108	2002	Hotels and restaurants (1) [61]	Accreditation of prior learning certification and validation of qualifications (competencies)	A.R.G.O. – Human resource accreditation to guarantee employability	http://leonardo. cec.eu.int/pdb/ Detail_En_2000. cfm?Numero=2120 221&Annee=2002
113	2002	Hotels and restaurants (1) [214] [237]	Certification and validation of qualifications (competencies) equal opportunities training modules	EU-EQT – European further training in tourism management. Investigating ways of incorporating European qualifications into national vocational training systems	http://leonardo. cec.eu.int/pdb/ Detail_En_2000. cfm?Numero=2112 670&Annee=2002
119	2002	Land transport; transport via pipelines (3) [135] [157]	Certification and validation of qualifications (competencies) curricula development	EUROWELD – European Certification of Welding Personnel	http://leonardo. cec.eu.int/pdb/ Detail_En_2000. cfm?Numero=2082 200&Annee=2002
122	2002	Manufacture of basic metals (1) [62]	Certification and validation of qualifications (competencies) skills assessment	Partnership for competency evaluation	http://leonardo. cec.eu.int/pdb/ Detail_En_2000. cfm?Numero=2115 825&Annee=2002
123	2002	Manufacture of basic metals (1) [138] [159]	Curricula development training modules new job profiles	TransPIB – New further training modules and new occupations in Europe – development of transnational vocational training	http://leonardo. cec.eu.int/pdb/ Detail_En_2000. cfm?Numero=2115 825&Annee=2002

N°	Year	Sector	Theme/task	Title	Web Page
134	2002	Manufacture of fabricated metal products, except machinery and equipment (1) [47] [158]	Continuous training skills assessment	CONTINUED – Continuing education of welding engineering and welding inspection personnel	http://leonardo.cec.eu.int/pdb/Detail_En_2000.cfm?Numero=2123226&Annee=2002
135	2002	Manufacture of fabricated metal products, except machinery and equipment (1) [119] [157]	Certification and validation of qualifications (competencies) curricula development	EUROWELD – European certification of welding personnel	http://leonardo.cec.eu.int/pdb/Detail_En_2000.cfm?Numero=2123226&Annee=2002
179	2002	Other business activities (1) [207]	Certification and validation of qualifications (competencies) skills assessment	CERTIDoc: European certification in information-documentation	http://leonardo.cec.eu.int/pdb/Detail_En_2000.cfm?Numero=2118036&Annee=2002
207	2002	Other service activities (2) [179]	Certification and validation of qualifications (competencies) skills assessment	CERTIDoc: European certification in information-documentation	http://leonardo.cec.eu.int/pdb/Detail_En_2000.cfm?Numero=2118036&Annee=2002
219	2002	Post and telecommunications (2) [78]	Accreditation of prior learning skills assessment	AKS – Development of methodology and systems for validation of accumulated knowledge and skills (AKS)	http://leonardo.cec.eu.int/pdb/Detail_En_2000.cfm?Numero=2131005&Annee=2002
220	2002	Private households with employed persons (2) [95]	Training modules skills assessment	Home-care in Europe – flexible vocational training of home-nurses within the European health care area, where acquired skills will be recognised through validation	http://leonardo.cec.eu.int/pdb/Detail_En_2000.cfm?Numero=2127021&Annee=2002

N°	Year	Sector	Theme/task	Title	Web Page
244	2002	Research and development (1) [74] [194]	Certification and validation of qualifications (competencies) new job profiles training of trainers	eNSTRUCT – Preparing the new generation of trainers	http://leonardo. cec.eu.int/pdb/ Detail_En_2000. cfm?Numero=2114 064&Annee=2002
248	2002	Retail trade, except of motor vehicles and motorcycles; repair of personal and household goods	Certification and validation of qualifications (competencies) in-service training continuous training	Learning service – A skills development project in the services sector	http://leonardo. cec.eu.int/pdb/ Detail_En_2000. cfm?Numero=2112 644&Annee=2002
251	2002	Retail trade, except of motor vehicles and motorcycles; repair of personal and household goods (3) [17] [265]	Certification and validation of qualifications (competencies) continuous training cooperation between enterprises	E(CO)-QUALIFY – Introduction of ICT-supported further training for managers and employees in ecological product retail, and development of European training standards	http://leonardo. cec.eu.int/pdb/ Detail_En_2000. cfm?Numero=2112 674&Annee=2002

Cedefop
(European Centre for the Development of Vocational Training)

Typology of knowledge, skills and competences: clarification of the concept and prototype

Jonathan Winterton
Françoise Delamare - Le Deist
Emma Stringfellow

Luxembourg: Office for Official Publications of the European Communities

2006 – 131 pp. – 17.5x25 cm

(Cedefop Reference series; 64 – ISSN 1608-7089)

ISBN 92-896-0427-1

Cat. No: TI-73-05-526-EN-C

Price (excluding VAT) in Luxembourg: EUR 25

No of publication: 3048 EN